3 Crucial
Questions
about
the Last Days

3 Crucial Questions
Grant R. Osborne and Richard J. Jones, Jr., editors

Other Books by Daniel J. Lewis

3 Crucial
Questions
about
the Last Days

Daniel J. Lewis

Baker Books

A Division of Baker Book House Co
Grand Rapids, Michigan 49516

© 1998 by Daniel J. Lewis

Published by Baker Books
a division of Baker Book House Company
P.O. Box 6287, Grand Rapids, MI 49516-6287

Printed in the United States of America

Library of Congress Cataloging-in-Publication Data

Lewis, Daniel J., 1950–
    3 crucial questions about the last days / Daniel J. Lewis.
      p.   cm.
    Includes bibliographical references and index.
    ISBN 0-8010-5820-1 (pbk.)
    1. End of the world. I. Title.
BT876.L48   1998
236'.9–dc21
                                      98-23845
                                         CIP

For information about academic books, resources for Christian leaders, and all new releases available from Baker Book House, visit our web site:
http://www.bakerbooks.com

To my sons,
James, Travis, and Chad,
who have enriched my life
beyond measure

❖

Contents

❖

Illustrations

❖

Editors' Preface

T he books in the 3 Crucial Questions series are the published form of the 3 Crucial Questions Seminars, which are sponsored by Bridge Ministries of Detroit, Michigan. The seminars and books are designed to greatly enhance your Christian walk. The following comments will help you appreciate the unique features of the book series.

The 3 Crucial Questions series is based on two fundamental observations. First, there are crucial questions related to the Christian faith for which imperfect Christians seem to have no final answers. Christians living in eternal glory may know fully even as they are known by God, but now we know only in part (1 Cor. 13:12). Therefore, we must ever return to such questions with the prayer that God the Holy Spirit will continue to lead us nearer to "the truth, the whole truth, and nothing but the truth." While recognizing their own frailty, the authors contributing to this series pray that they are thus led.

Second, each Christian generation partly affirms its solidarity with the Christian past by reaffirming "the faith which was once delivered unto the saints" (Jude 3 KJV). Such an affirmation is usually attempted by religious scholars who are notorious for talking only to themselves or by nonexperts whose grasp of the faith lacks depth of insight. Both situations are unfortunate, but we feel that our team of contributing authors is well prepared to avoid them. Each author is a competent Christian scholar able to share tremendous learning in down-to-earth language both laity and experts can appreciate. In a word, you have in hand a book that is part of a rare series, one that is neither pedantic nor pediatric.

The topics addressed in the series have been chosen for their timelessness, interest level, and importance to Christians everywhere. And the contributing authors are committed to discussing them in a manner that promotes Christian unity. Thus, they discuss not only areas of disagreement among Christians but significant areas of agreement as well. Seeking peace and pursuing it as the Bible commands (1 Peter 3:11), they stress common ground on which Christians with different views may meet for wholesome dialogue and reconciliation.

The books in the series consist not merely of printed words; they consist of words to live by. Their pages are filled not only with good information but with sound instruction in successful Christian living. For study is truly Christian only when, in addition to helping us understand our faith, it helps us to live our faith. We pray therefore that you will allow God to use the 3 Crucial Questions series to augment your growth in the grace and knowledge of our Lord and Savior Jesus Christ.

Grant R. Osborne
Richard J. Jones, Jr.

❖

Acknowledgments

This book is an expansion of lectures given under the auspices of Bridge Ministries at Madonna University, Detroit, Michigan, in September 1996. Special thanks are due to several people who graciously consented to read the manuscript, and who made many valuable suggestions. These include David Jones, Moffat College of Bible, Africa Inland Mission; Daniel B. Clendenin, InterVarsity Graduate Student Fellowship, Stanford University; Phil Leage, School of Biblical Studies, University of the Nations, Nuneaton, England; Rod Loudermilk, All Saints Evangelical Orthodox Mission, Acworth, Georgia; Dan Scott, senior pastor, Valley Cathedral, Phoenix, Arizona; Jonathan C. Enright, associate pastor, Troy Christian Chapel; Ray Wiersma, senior editor, Baker Book House; and of course the series editors, Richard J. Jones, Jr., Bridge Ministries, Detroit, Michigan; and Grant R. Osborne, Trinity Evangelical Divinity School, Deerfield, Illinois. Their assistance brought greater clarity to the subject and enabled me to avoid several errors. Above all, their Christian diversity helped make the manuscript as even-handed as possible. Any remaining errors or unevenness is my responsibility.

❖

Abbreviations

ASV	American Standard Version
JB	Jerusalem Bible
KJV	King James Version
mg	margin
NAB	New American Bible
NASB	New American Standard Bible
NEB	New English Bible
NIV	New International Version
NKJV	New King James Version
Phillips	The New Testament in Modern English (J. B. Phillips)
RSV	Revised Standard Version
RV	Revised Version
TEV	Today's English Version
Weymouth	The New Testament in Modern Speech (Richard Francis Weymouth)
Williams	The New Testament in Plain English (Charles Kingsley Williams)

❖

Introduction

large banner hangs over the entrance to the Old Royal Observatory in Greenwich, England, where an atomic clock sets the standard for all the timepieces in the world. The banner reads, "The Millennium Starts Here: 2000." By conventional thinking, at midnight on December 31, 1999, the human race will begin a new millennium.[1] Humans are accustomed to paying special attention to time, of course—birthdays, anniversaries, decades, and centennials—but the sheer immensity of a millennium is sobering. Since the end of the prehistoric period and the beginning of the historical period at around 3000 B.C., there have been only five such transitions. How many more will there be? No one knows, but there are many people who believe the next one will be the last—and a few even have doubts that the world will survive long enough to see it!

Such a viewpoint is hardly novel. For years new predictions have been offered, innovative interpretations of the Bible printed and distributed, and fresh calculations issued to convince, if not the population at large, at least the Christian community, that time is running out. In the early 1800s many believed Napoleon was the Antichrist. During World War I Kaiser Wilhelm was so regarded on the basis of a specious treatment of Zechariah 11:17. In World War II it was Adolf Hitler and Benito Mussolini. The Cold War period witnessed suggestions like Nikita Khrushchev and his successors, John F. Kennedy, or Fidel Castro. The late 1960s and early 1970s, and especially the period of the Six-Day War between Israel and Egypt, were awash with predictions. Preachers branded the European Common Market (now the European Union) as the revived Roman Empire, a federation of nations that would become the kingdom of the beast (Rev. 13). Popular writers like Hal Lindsey, whose *Late Great Planet Earth* was the best-selling nonfiction book of the 1970s, took current

15

world politics and translated them into plausible scenarios from the books of Ezekiel, Daniel, and Revelation. In 1982 the alignment of the planets within the same quadrant of our solar system convinced many that we were on the threshold of the apocalypse. In the late 1980s Edgar Whisenant published eighty-eight reasons why 1988 looked like the year of the church's rapture. When nothing happened, he published another work explaining "what went wrong in 1988—and why," but it was hardly a retraction. Rather, it was a defense of his original thesis with minor adjustments pointing to 1989 instead.

Speculation regarding Christ's return shows no sign of abating. With machine-gun rapidity, a mass of pamphlets, tracts, articles, and books about the last days keep rolling from the presses, so that one might expect an eventual saturation point, but not so. Radio evangelist Harold Camping, president of Family Radio, went public in September 1992 with a prediction that September 1994 would see the skies darken at midday and graves would open. In 1994 the Southwest Radio Church reported that yeshivas throughout Jerusalem were training priests and Levites for resuming sacrificial worship as a fulfilment of the last nine chapters of Ezekiel. These are a bare sampling of the scores of predictions and interpretations that have appeared.[2] With the transition in millennia, no one should expect the stream of speculation to dry up!

Even Christians from the postapostolic church were prone to make predictions regarding the second coming of Jesus. Hippolytus of Rome (170–236) predicted the world would end in A.D. 500. Near the end of the first millennium A.D. many Christians believed that they were living in the final days of the age. The visions in the Revelation of John heralding the end of the age have been taken to refer to the Muslims, Genghis Khan, the Roman Catholics, the Protestants, the Bolsheviks, and almost every other significant world power, religious or political.

Many conservative Protestant Christians have grown up on a steady diet of colored charts which purport to explain the mysteries of the last things. Some believe that the notes in the Scofield Reference Bible, the most influential publication for disseminating dispensational ideas, have almost the same validity as does the scriptural text itself. Though in the seventeenth and eighteenth centuries the historicist view of the Book of Revelation as a depiction of church history from the apostolic period to the end of time prevailed, the twentieth century has seen a complete turnaround. Today many conservative Christians have grown up under the system of dispensationalism with its emphasis on the future of geopolitical Israel. Whereas four hundred years ago Christians wrangled over whether the seven-headed beast in Revelation was Martin Luther or the pope, in this century they wrangle over whether the rapture will take place before or after the tribulation. In the past half century the eschatological profile of evangelicals has become even more diverse. C. I. Scofield and the older dispensationalists no longer hold the power that they once wielded. Amillennialism and historic premillennialism have gained in respectability. Postmillennialism, which almost died after the two world wars, has made a modest comeback.

One reason such widely divergent opinions exist is that many fail to take into account the historical background of the Old Testament prophets. Only after we have stood in the sandals of the Old Testament believer are we really ready to take up the staff of the New Testament Christian—and only then can we intelligently address the crucial questions about the last days. This book aims at correcting the negligence. While it will not answer all the questions raised by the various systems of prophetic interpretation, it will explore three crucial questions about the last days from the standpoint of biblical theology: (1) Are we in the last days? (2) Should Christians try to predict Christ's return? and (3) What must Christians believe about the last days?

Before launching into these questions, however, we must lay out briefly the historical milieu in which the Hebrew prophets wrote. Without such knowledge the interpreter is bound to arrive at conclusions that are foreign to the biblical text. Understanding the Old Testament background will provide some balance for Christians who feel overwhelmed and confused by the multitude of viewpoints. Our approach will be both scholarly and pastoral, for the three crucial questions are practical as well as academic. Finally, it is hoped that this volume will persuade Christians that the center of the church's faith cannot be any eschatological system per se. This is not to say that eschatology is dispensable, but that no scheme of eschatology should stand at the center of one's faith. There is a center, but it is the cross and resurrection of Jesus, not a speculative calendar about the end of the world.

The Framework of Biblical Theology

To answer questions such as the ones posed by this book, it is critically important to work within the framework of biblical theology, especially Old Testament theology, which has been sorely neglected. Unlike systematic theology, which combines biblical passages into generalized doctrines, or historical theology, which surveys the history of Christian thought, biblical theology is rooted in the immediate context of the biblical documents. It pays attention to the literary genre, era, historical circumstances, and overall flow of thought of a given book or author. Such a method, while it does not follow the more familiar path of Western logical synthesis, has the advantage of addressing the prophetic ideas of the Scripture as they arose in their own historical context. This context must not be passed over as superfluous, for if one is to perceive what the New Testament teaches about the last days, one must first take account of those forces that shaped this hope in the writings of the ancient Hebrew prophets. Failure to do so results in an artificial hermeneutic— a ouija-board approach to the Bible—which selects phrases or verses here and there, pasting them together into a collage which tends to stray from the original meaning of the biblical writers.[3]

A firm grasp of the historical framework is essential, then, before any real progress can be made in answering prophetic questions. For the notion of the last days originates not in some abstract discussion about the end of history, but in the historical vicissitudes of Israel's rise and fall. To seek to answer such questions outside this context flies in the face of any sound understanding of the prophets.

Given the importance of biblical theology, anyone who wishes to pose questions concerning the last days must begin with the writing prophets, for it is in their oracles that the vocabulary of the last days developed. Furthermore, one cannot examine these prophets while bracketing out their times, for they preached in the midst of the push and pull of politics in the ancient world. To short-circuit this historical and contextual framework is to undermine the interpretive effort.

Linear History and God's Lordship over Time

To understand what the Bible teaches about the last days, the interpreter must be aware of the biblical concept of linear time. Time, as the Bible depicts it, falls into the categories of past ("formerly"), present ("now"), and future ("then"). While Holy Scripture commences with the majestic phrase "in the beginning" (Gen. 1:1), time will be consummated at some future point when, as Paul says, "the end will come" (1 Cor. 15:24). This assumption of linear time, which lies behind the entire concept of promise that is so central to the covenants God made with Abraham, Moses, and David, makes prophetic thought possible. Beginning in the earliest stories of Genesis, the assumption of linear time is consistent throughout the Old Testament and essential to the language of fulfilment, which plays such a critical role in the Gospels.

God, who is the sovereign Lord of history, superintends time. He bends history to his own purposes, as aptly illustrated in the Joseph stories (Gen. 45:4–8; 50:19–21). Furthermore, God has a purpose in history. While the nations surrounding Israel were oblivious to God's purpose (Mic. 4:12), the Lord revealed it through his prophets (Amos 3:7). Especially in the latter oracles of the Book of Isaiah, God's repeated assertion that no one is like unto him aims at elucidating his hidden but all-powerful purposes in history (Isa. 40:25; 41:26–28; 42:9; 44:6–8, 24–28; 45:21; 46:8–11; 48:3–6).

In revealing God's future purposes, the prophets sometimes predicted events in the near future and sometimes events in the far future. It is critically important that the interpreter determine which of the two a particular oracle addresses. One mistake prophecy buffs often make is misinterpreting prophecies of the near future in a millennial way.

The Covenantal Tension

In addition to being aware of linear history and God's superintendence of it, it is essential, prior to any discussion about the last days, to appreciate the covenantal framework out of which the prophets wrote. In the ancient Near East the covenant was an important social relationship that bound together nations, families, and individuals. A covenant between two parties was a binding agreement, often with conditions attached. Early in Genesis, God began using the social institution of covenant to establish a lasting relationship with the family of Abraham. What the prophets later said about the last days has roots in the covenants that God established respectively with Abraham, Moses, and David. Alongside these covenants were two historical events between which the sacred history of the Old Testament moved: the exodus of Israel from Egypt to Canaan and the exile of Israel from Canaan to Mesopotamia. The fulfilment of God's promise in the exodus and conquest of Canaan and its retraction in the exile became the ground for the vision of the last days.

In the first covenant, God promised blessing and progeny to Abram (Gen. 12:1–3). In particular, his family was to receive the land of Canaan as a divine grant (Gen. 15:18–21; 17:1–8). The exodus and conquest made this promise a reality (Exod. 6:6–8). The promises of the land in the covenant with Abraham are most significant (Gen. 12:7; 13:14–17; 15:18–21; 17:8; 22:17b; 26:3–4; 28:13; 35:12). Not only were they couched in the language of a grant, they were considered to be effective forever. The event of the exodus was a fulfilment of these promises of land, given on oath by God to Abraham (Exod. 3:16–17; 6:2–8; 32:13; 33:1; Num. 32:11; Deut. 1:8; 6:10; 9:5; 30:20; 34:4).

In the second covenant there were also solemn statements about the land. However, there was also a significant shift. The Pentateuch contained the inexorable Deuteronomic code of blessings for obedience and cursings for disobedience (Deut. 27–30). In the Abrahamic covenant, the promises of land were given perpetually. In the Mosaic covenant, the land was given conditionally. The Deuteronomic code became the theological determinant for Israel's national history. Disobedience not only prohibited the original group from entering the land immediately at Kadesh (Num. 14:40–45), but canceled entirely their personal participation in any future fulfilment (Num. 14:22–23; 32:6–13; Josh. 5:6). Thus possession of the land was not unconditional; in fact, the land could be lost (Lev. 26:32–35, 38–39; Deut. 28:36, 49–52, 64–68; 29:27–28).

The conquest under Joshua was a fulfilment of the land grant (Josh. 1:6; Judg. 2:1), and references to "the land" are copious in the Book of Joshua. However, it is apparent that possession of the land was far more tied to the Deuteronomic blessings and cursings than to any unconditional guarantee. Joshua's farewell address (Josh. 23:12–16), the covenant renewal at Shechem (Josh. 24:13, 20), the political turmoil during the period of the tribal league (Book of Judges), the Philistine threat during the time of Eli and Samuel (Book of 1 Samuel), the dedicatory prayer of Solomon (1 Kings 8:33–34, 46–51), and finally, the exile of the northern and southern nations (2 Kings 17, 25) all point toward the conditionality of land possession.

In the third covenant God gave yet further promises concerning the land. It was not until the wars of David that the conquest of Canaan was complete. Israel's political fortunes had seesawed back and forth until, in the time of Eli and Samuel, the nation's very existence was threatened. When David gained control, he quickly mobilized his army to annex Jerusalem and bring the Philistine threat to an end (2 Sam. 5:6–25). At last, when the nation was secure, David determined to construct a permanent place for the ark in accordance with the ancient expectations voiced in the Pentateuch (2 Sam. 7:1–2; Deut. 12). This idea of permanency had powerful symbolic value. The temple contrasted sharply with the temporary character of the tabernacle and the more or less temporary political character of the tribal league. The construction of a permanent house for the ark reflected the new security of the nation in the land and signaled the end of the conquest.

While Yahweh did not allow David the privilege of following through on this project, he did establish a covenant with David. This third covenant guaranteed to him a perpetual dynasty (2 Sam. 7:11b–16) and to the Israelite nation the land of Canaan, a homeland from which they would never be disturbed (2 Sam. 7:10–11a; 22:51b; 23:5a).

Just as the conditional covenant at Sinai created tension with the previously existing unconditional promises to Abraham, so the promissory oath to David created tension with the previously existing conditional land grants of the Mosaic covenant. On the one hand, the Deuteronomic blessings and cursings seemed to make possession of the land conditional. On the other hand, the sure promise to David seemed to guarantee possession of the land unconditionally. The exodus and the exile graphically demonstrate these tensions. In the exodus and conquest the promises of land were fulfilled, but in the exile the land was taken away. How the land was lost is critical to a sound understanding of the prophetic vision for the last days.

Figure 1.1

Two Historical Polarities

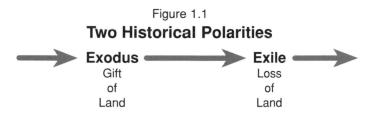

Exodus	Exile
Gift	Loss
of	of
Land	Land

The Covenants and the History of Post-Davidic Israel

After the death of Solomon the united monarchy ruptured, never to be brought together again. The northern kingdom turned away from the Davidic covenant, apparently deciding that it was invalid (1 Kings 12:16). The northern citizens reverted to the older, pre-Davidic ways and returned to the ancient pattern of worship at various local shrines (Judg. 18:28b–30; 1 Kings 12:26–33; Amos 4:4; 5:4–5; 8:14). At the secession they bluntly said, "What share do we have in David, what part in Jesse's son? To your tents, O Israel! Look after your own house, O David" (1 Kings 12:16b)! Still, they insisted that the land of the northern kingdom should be theirs perpetually, since it had been given to Abraham by grant. For the north the Abrahamic covenant was supreme, while the Davidic covenant was rejected.

The southern two tribes, on the other hand, remained faithful to David's dynasty and the Davidic covenant. Zion, the mountain on which Solomon's temple stood, was the central shrine for the south and remained so until the destruction of Jerusalem in 586 B.C.

In both north and south there was a stubborn optimism that the land was secure forever. Neither nation was willing to take seriously the blessings and cursings of the Deuteronomic code. The prophets inveighed against this smug overconfidence. These doomsters announced that the people, their cults, and the kings of Israel faced a most formidable antagonist, Yahweh himself. Amos and Hosea in the north and Isaiah and Micah in the south delivered a scathing message to their fellow citizens that both kingdoms were under divine judgment (Amos 2:4–16; Hos. 2:2–13; Isa. 3:1–4:1; Mic. 1:2–7). The pronouncements of the writing prophets called the two kingdoms to account through the covenant of Moses, especially in terms of the Deuteronomic blessings and cursings. There was no unconditional security for the land or the Davidic king!

Of course, such a message was unwelcome. Many, if not most Israelites, refused to believe until it was too late. In the north it was assumed that the ancient shrines of the patriarchs would be divinely protected, while in the south the longevity of the nation was believed to be guaranteed because the people had remained faithful to the dynasty of David. Countering this optimism, however, Amos declared that the shrines in the north were not safe (Amos 5:4–6). The northern kingdom would come under judgment because of flagrant disobedience (Amos 2:6–16). Contrary to popular opinion (Amos 7:10–13), the land was not unconditionally secure (Amos 3:11–12; Hos. 8:14). The people could and would be removed from the land (Amos 4:2–3; 7:11; Hos. 5:14; 9:17), and much of the population would be destroyed (Amos 5:3; 6:8–10; Hos. 10:13–15). The complacent citizens of northern Israel would come face to face with the terrible judgment of God within history (Amos 5:18–19; 6:1; 9:1–4; Hos. 13:7–9).

Though the southern kingdom lasted nearly a century and a half longer than her northern counterpart, Judah, too, was a kingdom under judgment (Isa. 3:13–14). In the south Micah bitterly opposed the voices which guaranteed peace and security (Mic. 2:6–7; 3:9–12). While there were brief periods of spiritual renewal and reform spearheaded by Hezekiah and Josiah (2 Chron. 29–31, 34–35), such efforts were too little too late (2 Kings 20:21; 21:9; 23:29–32). The prophets predicted that Jerusalem's false sense of security would be exposed to withering attack (Mic. 3:12; Isa. 28:18b–22; 29:1–4; Zeph. 1:2–7, 12). Yahweh's righteous anger would not be turned back (Isa. 5:25; 9:12b, 17b, 21b; 10:4b; 14:27). Of course, most people in the southern kingdom did not believe such a thing could happen (Mic. 3:11b; Jer. 22:21), and it is not unlikely that such warnings were treated as heresy (Mic. 2:6–7; Jer. 26:4–11). When the northern kingdom went into exile, its fall did not frighten those in Jerusalem (Jer. 3:6–10). The north had received no more than it deserved. Since the southern kingdom remained faithful to both David and the temple, was their security not guaranteed by God?

Not according to Jeremiah! The temple on Zion would be destroyed as surely as Shiloh had been razed in the days of Eli (Jer. 7:1–15)! Zephaniah as well as Jeremiah thundered out against this false security (Zeph. 1:12; Jer. 6:14; 8:11), for the temple on Zion was no guarantee of anything (Jer. 7:4, 9–11, 21–26). Furthermore, the Davidic dynasty would be swept away (Jer. 22:1–5, 21, 24–30; 36:30–31). To hope for a last-minute reprieve was utter folly (Jer. 21:1–7).

As long as Jerusalem was still standing and the exiled Davidic king Jehoiachin was still alive, many believed that the deportations to Babylon were only temporary hardships. Court prophets in Jerusalem predicted a quick reversal of Judah's fortunes (Jer. 28:1–4, 10–11). Among the exiles in Babylon there was also optimism. Thus when Ezekiel, a priest among the exiles, predicted that Jerusalem would be totally destroyed (Ezek. 7) and that God would vacate the temple on Zion (Ezek. 10:4–5, 18–19; 11:22–23), his compatriots dismissed his predictions as either false or irrelevant (Ezek. 12:21–22, 26–27; 20:49). False prophets continued to preach optimism (Jer. 6:14; 8:11; Ezek. 13:1–7, 10–12; cf. Jer. 29:15–23).

Such optimism notwithstanding, the doom of Jerusalem was sealed. The Babylonian armies again laid siege to Jerusalem, and this time the city was completely devastated. The temple was burned, and all the valuable and sacred objects were looted (2 Kings 25:1–21). A second deportation took from Jerusalem many of the remaining citizens (2 Chron. 36:20; Jer. 39:9–10; 52:24–27). This scattering of the Israelites among the nations was the direct fulfilment of the Deuteronomic code.

The difficulty of trying to reconcile the apparent unconditional character of the Davidic covenant with the realities of history is sharply evident in Psalm 89, especially in the transition between 89:19–37 and 89:38–51. After detailing the promises that Yahweh would establish David's throne and kingdom forever, the poet makes the wrenching observation, "But you have rejected, you have spurned, . . . you have renounced the covenant with your servant" (vv. 38–39). He then poses the haunting question, "How long, O Yahweh? Will you hide yourself forever? . . . Where is your former great love, which in your faithfulness you swore to David?" (vv. 46, 49). Where, indeed?

The Covenants and Hope beyond Exile

While it was the prophets who warned the Israelites of coming exile, it was also the prophets who called the remnant to look toward the future with hope. Exile, while it was God's strange therapy (Isa. 28:21–22), was not his last word. Even the Deuteronomic code spelled out the possibility of restoration after Israel had been scattered among the nations (Deut. 30:1–10). This theme of restoration resounds in the oracles of the prophets again and again.

The eighth-century prophets were the first to promise that a remnant would return from exile (Amos 9:13–15; Hos. 1:10–11; 2:21–23; 11:10–11; Isa. 10:20–22; 11:11–12, 16; Mic. 2:12–13; 4:6–8; 7:8–11). Isaiah of Jerusalem even named one of his sons Shear-Jashub ("a remnant will return") as a sign of this hopeful future (Isa. 7:3). The prophets of the seventh century continued the predictions of the regathering and restoration of the people to the land following judgment (Zeph. 3:20; Jer. 30:1–3; 31:16–17, 21–25; 33:7, 10–26; 50:18–19). As a sign that the land would once more belong to the Israelites, Yahweh instructed Jeremiah to buy a piece of property near Jerusalem, sealing the deed for the future (Jer. 32:6–15, 36–44). In addition, Jeremiah specified the length of the exile to be seventy years (Jer. 25:8–14; 29:10–14).

In the sixth century, Ezekiel preached to the exiles in Babylon that there was yet a future for Israel in the land (Ezek. 11:16–17; 20:34–38, 41–42; 34:11–16; 36:24, 28, 33–38; 37:12–14, 20–21; 39:25–29). Though Jerusalem was utterly devastated, in a relatively short time the exiles would be allowed to go back home (Ezek. 36:8–12; cf. Isa. 40:1–2). Surprisingly, a messiah would arise in the form of a non-Israelite: Cyrus, the king of Persia, would allow the people to return (Isa. 41:2b–4, 25; 44:28; 45:1, 4, 13).

Associated with the predictions of a return from exile were breathtaking promises about a new commonwealth for Jerusalem and the land of Israel. Idolatry would be purged (Ezek. 11:18; 37:23), divine forgiveness would be extended (Isa. 44:21–23; Jer. 31:34; 33:8; 50:20; Ezek. 36:25–26, 29, 33), and the gift of the Holy Spirit would be poured out (Isa. 32:15; 44:3; 59:20–21; Ezek. 11:19–20; 36:27; 37:14, 23; 39:29; Joel 2:28–32). A new covenant would be established (Jer. 31:31–34; 32:40–41; Ezek. 16:60, 62; 34:25; 37:26), and a new Davidic king would rule in justice (Isa. 55:3–5; Jer. 23:5–6; 30:8–9; 33:17–26; Ezek. 34:23–24; 37:24–25). No longer would there be northern and southern Israelite kingdoms, but Israel would be united forever (Hos. 1:11; Ezek. 37:15–23). New tribal divisions would be made (Ezek. 47:13–48:29) so that the entire people of Israel could surround a rebuilt Jerusalem (Isa. 44:24–26; 45:13; 52:1–12; 54:11–17; 61:4–6; Jer. 31:38–40; Ezek. 36:33, 36, 38) and a second temple (Isa. 44:28; Ezek. 37:26; 40–43; Joel 2:32). Mount Zion would become the spiritual cen-

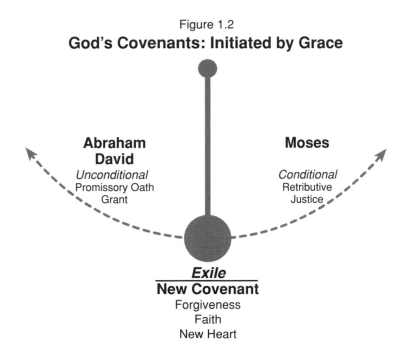

Figure 1.2
God's Covenants: Initiated by Grace

Abraham   **Moses**
David
Unconditional   *Conditional*
Promissory Oath   Retributive
Grant   Justice

Exile
New Covenant
Forgiveness
Faith
New Heart

ter for the nations of the earth (Isa. 2:2–4; 49:14–23; 51:3–6; 60; 62; Mic. 4:1–2). Crops would thrive (Amos 9:13; Hos. 2:21–22; Isa. 41:17–20; Ezek. 34:26–29; 36:29–30, 34–35). No longer would there be war (Isa. 2:4; Mic. 4:3) but universal peace (Isa. 11:6–9). There was indeed a new future for the nation! The nature and range of this new future are at the heart of the affirmations in Isaiah 40–66.

After the Persians swallowed up the Babylonian Empire, Cyrus, in his first regnal year over Babylon (538 B.C.), issued a decree authorizing the repatriation of the exiles (2 Chron. 36:22–23; Ezra 1:2–4; 6:3–5). Shesh-bazzar, the leader of the returning group, was permitted to take with him the holy vessels of the temple which had been looted several decades earlier (Ezra 1:7–11; 5:13–15; 6:5).

The Disillusionment of the Postexilic Community

The dreams of the exiles returning from Babylon were built upon the glorious promises of restoration given by the earlier prophets. The opening of Psalm 126 captures the jubilant mood of those who made the trek westward from Babylon (see Ezra 2:64; Neh. 7:66). However, the first blush of excitement soon degenerated into disillusionment. Though both

Sheshbazzar and his colleague Zerubbabel were in the lineage of David, they were hardly the stuff to fulfil the dazzling promises of a Davidic king who would rule Israel as a jewel among the nations of the world. And certainly the ruins of Jerusalem did not qualify as the spiritual center for all nations. The great altar for sacrifice was erected (Ezra 3:1–6), but even this was achieved only in an atmosphere of intimidation (Ezra 3:3a). It was a tribute to the Jews' courage that the altar was completed at all.

Pressing ahead under the governorship of Zerubbabel and the spiritual influence of Joshua the son of Jozadak, the people began the foundation for the new temple (Ezra 3:7–11). The base for the new edifice was a far cry from the temple envisioned by Ezekiel, however, and those who could still remember the first temple wept with disappointment (Ezra 3:12–13; Hag. 2:3). When the local populace offered to help, they were turned down abruptly (Ezra 4:1–3). For spite, they set about discouraging and intimidating those who were trying to finish the temple (Ezra 4:4–5). Since the rebuffed locals were remnants of the northern tribes, it is clear that the vision of a united Israel would not materialize at this time. In the end, construction came to a standstill. It remained checked for the balance of Cyrus's rule, for that of his successor, Cambyses II (530–522), and on into the rule of Darius I (Ezra 4:24).

The times were particularly discouraging. The community of returned exiles combated a series of droughts and crop failures, which in turn produced economic hardship (Hag. 1:6, 9–11; 2:15–17, 19). It was indeed a day of "small things" (Zech. 4:10), and within a few years the governor of the Trans-Euphrates region of Persia could not even remember Cyrus's edict giving permission for the Jews to rebuild their temple (Ezra 5:3–4). An archival search had to be made before the work could continue (Ezra 5:5–6:12). It is not surprising that the people were ready to give up altogether (Hag. 1:2). They needed spiritual focus and leadership, a crisis to which the prophets Haggai and Zechariah responded.

It is apparent that by the time of Malachi the second temple had been completed (Mal. 1:10; 3:1, 10). It is also apparent that the temple rituals had lapsed into perfunctory acts which were performed with laxity and contempt for Torah's requirements (Mal. 1:13–14; 3:8–9, 13–14). The people were bitterly disillusioned. Some wept (Mal. 2:13), while others were cynical and hostile toward Yahweh (Mal. 1:2; 2:17; 3:7–8, 13–14). The sins of occultism, adultery, perjury, exploitation, and discrimination flourished as once they had flourished among the people before the exile (Mal. 3:5). Some of the people were entering into mixed marriages with unbelievers (Mal. 2:11–12; cf. Neh. 13:23–31), and the priests of the temple were failing in their duties of moral instruction

(Mal. 2:7–8). The oracles of Malachi end with the promise of the coming of Elijah before the day of the Lord (Mal. 4:5–6).

The Ground of Eschatology

One cannot properly understand what the Bible says about the last days unless one understands what it says about the past, and in particular the concept of the last days that arose within the context of the ancient hope of Israel. The foregoing survey of Israel's history is intended as background to the view that the ground of biblical eschatology is the covenantal tension between the seemingly unconditional promises made to Abraham and David and the harsh conditionality of the Deuteronomic blessings and cursings given through Moses. This eschatological view assumes that in spite of the tragedy of exile and the precarious existence of the nation after the remnant returned from exile, the future still held the fulfillment of the promises made to Abraham and David. The disillusionment following the return from exile stands sharply etched against the messianic hope for the future. None of God's promises would fall to the ground!

At the same time the exile demanded that these bright promises be interpreted in a new way. The old hope that the kingdom of Israel would be the kingdom of God had been dashed to pieces. In its place were the prophetic voices that looked to the future for divine intervention, a future that, to echo Paul's phrase, was often seen as a "dim reflection." To those prophetic voices and their insight into the future we now turn.

Are We Living
in the Last Days?

The Old Testament Vision of the Last Days

Our opening chapter will build upon the sketch of Israel's history in the introduction, and especially upon the message of the prophets concerning the last days. It will require some patience on the part of the reader. It is not uncommon for interpreters to begin their study of prophecy in the New Testament and to turn back to the Old Testament only for brief excursions. This method is wrong! Rather, the interpreter should begin in the Old Testament and move forward so that the New Testament becomes the climax, for this is the way Jesus and the apostles necessarily had to work. This was, in fact, the approach he took with the two disciples at Emmaus: "Beginning with Moses and all the Prophets, he explained to them what was said in all the Scriptures concerning himself" (Luke 24:27). If one is not accustomed to doing theology in this way, it may seem nontraditional, but the rewards will be great!

There is a clear consensus among the New Testament writers that the beginning of the Christian Era marked the beginning of the last days. The apostles would have thought it strange to even pose the question that later generations ask, "Are we near the end?" For the apostles, the last days began with Jesus the Messiah—his earthly life, death, resurrection, and ascension to the Father's right hand. Understanding how they reached that conclusion is the goal of this chapter. We must begin, however, with the message of the Hebrew prophets who preceded them, for the New Testament writers did not invent the ideas and vocabulary relating to the last days. Rather, they employed language and thought forms passed down to them from the Old Testament. When the Hebrew prophets used the expression "the last days," they did so in the context of their pronouncements about "the day of Yahweh." These ancient phrases and concepts merit careful examination.

The Hebrew Prophets and "the Day of Yahweh"

The vocabulary relating to the last days essentially developed in the eighth century before Christ. To be sure, there are scattered hints of God's eschatological purposes in earlier documents of the Hebrew Bible. However, these expectations can only be described as vague. Not until the prophets began to actively predict that the nations of Israel and Judah would go into exile was the vocabulary of the last days defined and sustained.

In the eighth century B.C. arose a quartet of prophets with a startling consensus about Israel's future. Amos and Hosea preached an unrelenting message of judgment to the northern clans, while Isaiah and Micah did the same in the south. Against the popular theology of a guaranteed future, these spokesmen for God announced that as a fulfilment of the Deuteronomic curses for disobeying the Torah the nations of Israel and Judah would fall.

In the midst of these ominous predictions we meet a striking phrase— "the day of Yahweh" or "the day of the Lord." Amos's reference to the day of Yahweh in 5:18 suggests that the expression was already current. The Israelites had in mind that the day of Yahweh would be a time of blessing, prosperity, hope, and light. The phrase expressed Israel's hope for national success. Amos, by contrast, spoke of "that day" as the day of reckoning (2:16; 3:14).

It is likely that the day of Yahweh was probably viewed as the eschatological moment when Yahweh's victory over his enemies would culminate in the supremacy of Israel. What a shock, then, to hear Amos preach that "that day," far from being what was expected, would be a devastating judgment (Amos 5:18–20). The day of Yahweh was doomsday; when it arrived, the northern nation would meet a wrathful God (Amos 4:12). Yahweh was the divine lion, and Israel was his prey (Amos 3:4, 8, 12). Those who longed for the day of Yahweh, thinking it was a day of vindication, should think again! Woe to them! It will not be a day of light, but terrible darkness, a day when even the bravest warriors flee naked (Amos 2:16). The northern nation will be punished for its sins in the crucible of history (Amos 3:14). Corpses will be flung everywhere

(Amos 8:3). God will cause the sun to set at noon so the earth will be darkened at midday (Amos 8:9). Festivals will turn to funerals, and God will not relent (Amos 8:10–11). Those who paid allegiance to the shrines set up by Jeroboam I will faint from thirst, falling never to rise again (Amos 8:13–14). God will hunt them all the way to hell, if necessary, to carry out the judgment of the Deuteronomic code (Amos 9:1–4).

It is clear enough that Amos, like his contemporary Hosea, antici-pated the coming invasion of the Assyrians (Hos. 9:3; 10:5–7; 11:11). Barely twenty-five years later, the terrible predictions of these prophets came to pass. In 722 B.C. the northern nation collapsed before the armies of Shalmaneser V and his brother Sargon II. The historical account of the fall of Samaria spells out the reason: "Yahweh warned Israel and Judah through all his prophets and seers. . . . But they would not listen" (2 Kings 17:13–14). Therefore Yahweh "removed them from his presence, as he had warned through all his servants the prophets. So the people of Israel were taken from their homeland into exile in Assyria, and they are still there" (2 Kings 17:23).

One might suppose that the prediction and fulfilment of Israel's fall in the late eighth century exhausted Amos's vision of the day of Yahweh. Certainly he viewed the day of Yahweh as a time of terrible judgment in the near future. Certainly he recognized the folly of looking toward that day as though it would unqualifiedly assure triumph for Israel (Amos 9:10). Yet, in spite of the dire forecast, Amos said that there was also a future beyond judgment. Though the nation would be destroyed, its destruction would not be total (Amos 9:8). Though the conditional curses of the Mosaic covenant would catch up with the sinful nation, the sure promises of David would not disappear. Instead, "that day" would also include a restoration of David's "fallen tent" (Amos 9:11). So Amos's message of judgment was mitigated by a vision of hope. Judgment was not Yahweh's final word. Rather, the ultimate purposes of God involved blessing, even though that blessing might be pushed into an unknown future.

The day of Yahweh, then, was not merely a judgment within history in which the Assyrians overran the northern Israelite nation. It was also the threshold of restoration, unparalleled prosperity, and fulfilment of the Abrahamic and Davidic covenantal promises that the Israelites would be planted in their own land never to be uprooted again (Amos 9:11–15; Hos. 3:4–5; 11:10–11; 13:14; 14:4–9).

This same vision of judgment and hope is paradigmatic for the other prophets who describe the day of Yahweh. They, too, speak of both judg-ment and hope. For Joel the day of Yahweh was a time of terrible destruction, famine, and fire (Joel 1:15–20). Like Amos he saw it as a deadly invasion, a time of darkness and calamity (Joel 2:1–10). Whoever the invading force, and most interpreters agree that Joel like Amos refers to the Assyrians, they were the instruments of Yahweh's judgment, hence "his army" (Joel 2:11). At the same time Joel's vision of the future was broad enough to embrace blessing as well as judgment upon the nations. He predicted that before the "great and dreadful day of the LORD" the Holy Spirit will be poured out upon all people. Everyone who calls upon the Lord's name will be saved (Joel 2:28–32). Paradoxically, the day of Yahweh includes both judgment upon God's enemies and refuge for his people (Joel 3:14–16).

Thus the day of Yahweh has a broad semantic range. On the one hand, it can refer to a historical judgment as specific as the invasion by the Assyrians or Babylonians. On the other, it can refer to an indeterminate future far beyond the events of the exile. Isaiah in southern Israel could speak of the day of Yahweh as "a cruel day, with wrath and fierce anger" (Isa. 13:9). It would be a time of darkness and punishment for sin (Isa. 13:10–11), a day when God would bring low the arrogant power-brokers of the world (Isa. 2:12–21). A century later, Zephaniah, anticipating Babylon's attack upon Judah, similarly spoke of the day of the Lord as a period of darkness, gloom, invasion, and tragedy (Zeph. 1:14–18). Jeremiah (ch. 46) used the same metaphor to predict Pharaoh Neco's defeat by Nebuchadnezzar at Carchemish (605 B.C.), a defeat confirmed by the cuneiform Babylonian Chronicles. Ezekiel used "day of Yahweh" to refer to the fall of Israel (Ezek. 7:19), later to the fall of Jerusalem (Ezek. 13:5), and still later to the Babylonian invasion of Egypt (Ezek. 30:3–4). Obadiah saw it as the day of judgment upon all nations, but especially upon Edom because of its violence against Israel (Obad. 15; cf. Ps. 137:7).

While the vision of judgment is central, the day of Yahweh also embraces restoration following judgment. Edom would be burned like stubble, but the people of Israel would be delivered and restored to their land (Obad. 16–21). Zechariah, who prophesied after both Assyria and Babylon had been defeated, also saw the day of Yahweh as a time of both judgment and triumph. For him it was the invasion of all nations against Jerusalem, a crisis when God would defend Jerusalem against all comers (Zech. 14:1–2). Yahweh himself would fight for his holy city, defeating his enemies and elevating Jerusalem to be the capital of the world (Zech. 14:3–21). Finally, Malachi predicted that before the "great and dreadful day of Yahweh" the Lord would send Elijah the prophet to preach repentance (Mal. 4:5), a prediction the apostles understood to have been fulfilled in the ministry of John the Baptist (Matt. 17:10–13).

The fluidity of the expression "the day of Yahweh" is not unlike the English word "doomsday." It can refer to the last judgment, but in a lesser sense it can also refer to a dreaded day of reckoning within history. It was so used by the prophets of Israel. The day of Yahweh could refer to something as specific as the Assyrian and Babylonian invasions of the eighth and sixth centuries before Christ. It could encompass the historical defeats of Egypt and Edom. It could also anticipate a future restoration of God's people, the rise of the house of David, and, according to the New Testament, the events surrounding the coming of the Messiah. The day of Yahweh included both judgment and salvation—judgment upon God's enemies and salvation for his people.

The semantic range of the expression illustrates a defining principle for interpreting the eschatological predictions of the Hebrew prophets. The prophets employed a technique that we call double entendre, that is, their statements frequently embraced two meanings. The double meanings in their predictions might point to some well-defined threat in the relatively near future, but also some more ambiguous climax in the indeterminate future. One of the most famous double entendres is Nathan's prediction that David would have a son who would build God's

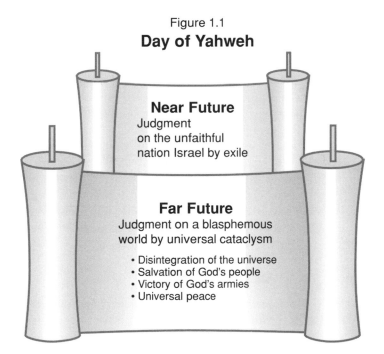

Figure 1.1
Day of Yahweh

Near Future
Judgment
on the unfaithful
nation Israel by exile

Far Future
Judgment on a blasphemous
world by universal cataclysm

- Disintegration of the universe
- Salvation of God's people
- Victory of God's armies
- Universal peace

house (2 Sam. 7:12–13). That son, of course, was Solomon. But did the concrete historical fulfilment in Solomon's erection of the first temple exhaust the meaning of the prophecy? Hardly, if one takes seriously the New Testament interpretation (see, e.g., Heb. 1:5b).

"The Last Days"

The phrase "the last days" takes on concrete meaning in the context of prophetic references to the coming day of Yahweh, for the day of Yahweh is virtually a synonym for the last days. To be sure, the Hebrew expression *bĕʾaḥărît hayyāmîm* ("in the days to come, at the end of days, in the last days") appeared earlier than the writing prophets in various predictions concerning Israel's future (Gen. 49:1; Num. 24:14; Deut. 4:30; 31:29). However, it was descriptions of the coming exile and of the trauma of the day of Yahweh that shaped "the last days" as a reference to the climax of history.

The expression *bĕʾaḥărît hayyāmîm,* like the day of Yahweh, carries with it a certain ambiguity. In one sense, it simply refers to events in the indeterminate future. However, a nuance suggesting the end of the age is also clearly present. Isaiah spoke of the establishment of Yahweh's temple "in the last days" as the center of worship for the nations (Isa. 2:2–4). This prediction was echoed by Micah, his contemporary (Mic. 4:1–5). Hosea predicted that "in the last days" the northern nation would return to God and David's family, whom they had rejected under Jeroboam I (Hos. 3:5). A century later Jeremiah predicted the restoration of the Moabites (Jer. 48:47) and the Elamites (Jer. 49:39) "in the last days," though he was careful to point out that the full meaning of God's purposes would not be known until such events could be assessed in retrospect (Jer. 23:20; 30:24). Ezekiel, Jeremiah's contemporary, predicted that "in the last days" the land of Israel would again suffer invasion, this time after the people had been restored from exile (Ezek. 38:8, 16). Daniel's cryptic predictions concerning the future also were given under the rubric of "the last days" (Dan. 2:28; 10:14). So definitive did the expression *bĕʾaḥărît hayyāmîm* become as a code word for the climax of the age that even the partial expression *ʾaḥărê-kēn* ("afterward") could be interpreted by Peter at Pentecost to mean "the last days" (Acts 2:17; cf. Joel 2:28).

Yahweh and the Nations

Was the Old Testament vision of the last days concerned exclusively with the Israelites? Not at all! An important aspect of this prophetic vision concerned nations other than Israel and Judah, a point that would not be lost on the writers in the New Testament. The anticipation of a historical climax was not limited to Israel's immediate geography. Rather Obadiah preached, "The Day of Yahweh is near for all nations" (Obad. 15–16). This day of God's reckoning, when "the arrogance of man will be brought low" (Isa. 2:12–17) and Zion will be elevated as an international center for worship, is to be universal in scope (Isa. 2:2–4; Mic. 4:1–5). The solar and stellar collapse accompanying the day of Yahweh will be a sign affecting the whole earth (Isa. 13:10; 24:23; 34:4; Ezek. 32:7; Joel 2:10, 30–31; 3:15).

Yahweh was not a provincial God, but, as the biblical poet put it, "his kingdom rules over all" (Ps. 103:19). Thus the prophets announced the judgment of God upon all the nations for their wickedness. Amos denounced Damascus, Ammon, and Moab for war crimes (Amos 1:3, 13; 2:1), and Philistia, Tyre, and Edom for slave trading (Amos 1:6, 9, 11). Isaiah condemned Assyria and Babylon for arrogance (Isa. 10:12; 13:1–14:27; 21:1–10). God's plan having been "determined for the whole world" and his hand being "stretched out over all nations" (Isa. 14:26; 34:1–15), Philistia, Moab, Damascus, Cush, Egypt, Arabia, and Tyre all faced divine judgment (Isa. 14:28–20:6; 21:11–17; 23:1–18). Jeremiah likewise predicted the defeat of Egypt, Philistia, Moab, Ammon, Edom, Damascus, Kedar, Hazor, Elam, and Babylon (Jer. 46–51). Ezekiel warned of the coming doom of Canaan, Phoenicia, and Egypt (Ezek. 25–32). Joel foresaw the arraignment of all the nations in the valley of judgment (Joel 3:1–17), and Zephaniah announced the ruin of Philistia, Moab, Ammon, Cush, and Assyria (Zeph. 2:4–15).

It is true, of course, that many of these judgments occurred in the wars of the eighth, seventh, and sixth centuries before Christ. Still, there is a futuristic tone to the predictions which is not exhausted by the rise and fall of kingdoms in the vicissitudes of ancient Near Eastern politics. Long after the trauma of the Assyrian and Babylonian invasions, Zechariah of the postexilic period warned of coming international war. Jeremiah's older prediction of a northern invasion by Babylon in the seventh century (Jer. 1:13–14; 4:6; 6:1, 22; 10:22; 13:20; 25:9, etc.) was only the prelude to yet another invasion from the north, this time by Yahweh who would march against the nations in judgment (Zech. 9:1–8). Warriors once more would invade Jerusalem (Zech. 12:1–9), but in the day of Yahweh, God himself would defend the city (Zech. 14:1–5, 12–15).

This vision about the nations also contained a striking paradox. Not only was there judgment, there was the added element of international conversion. The Philistines, once the perennial enemies of the tribe of Judah, would "become leaders in Judah" (Zech. 9:7). The survivors from all the nations would make an annual pilgrimage to Jerusalem to worship Yahweh and celebrate the feast of booths (Zech. 14:16–19). And in that day Yahweh would be king over the whole earth (Zech. 14:9).

The Remnant and the New Covenant

We have seen that the future envisioned by the prophets included both doomsday and salvation. We know that in the exile of Israel to Assyria and of Judah to Babylon the predictions of judgment were historically fulfilled. But to whom were the promises of blessing and salvation to be fulfilled? The Israelites had been marked for judgment, but who were the beneficiaries of the hope beyond judgment? Here the prophets introduce us to the concept of the remnant.

The Restoration of the Remnant

Just as the last days would bring war and judgment upon the nations of the world, they would also bring the restoration of God's remnant. The concept of a remnant was important to all the people of the ancient Near East, but especially to the Israelites. Against the background of war, famine, and forced migration there developed the notion of a group "left over."[1] This notion occurred quite early: in the Pentateuch it was already present in the narratives about the survivors of the great flood and the second generation of Israelites who entered Canaan. However, the idea really came into its own in light of the approaching exile of Israel and Judah. The hope for a remnant reconciled the seemingly unconditional promises to Abraham and David with the very conditional terms of the Mosaic covenant. The loss of the land was not forever, nor was the fall of David's dynasty without remedy. Although the unconditional promises had been foiled by the conditional curses of the Deuteronomic code, they still could be fulfilled to a future generation.

The prophets developed the remnant concept in association with the promises concerning the last days. From the northern Israelites would be saved a small scrap for the future (Amos 3:12; 5:3). Though judgment was coming to Judah, a remnant, a mere stump, would survive (Isa. 6:11–13; 10:22). To accentuate this hope, Isaiah named one of his sons Shear-Jashub, meaning "a remnant will return" (Isa. 7:3). So although Judah would be cut down like so many oaks (Isa. 6:13), yet from the stump of Jesse's family in Judah a small Branch would survive (Isa. 11:1). This Branch, an individual yet to be born, would be endowed by the Spirit of Yahweh to judge the nations and bring peace to the world (Isa. 11:2–9). The nations would rally to him. In addition, he would regather to their ancestral land a remnant of God's people who had been exiled to Assyria, Egypt, Babylon, and elsewhere (Isa. 11:10–16; see also 4:2–6). To Hezekiah, God even gave a sign that a remnant of Judah would survive (Isa. 37:30–32). To be sure, this remnant would be scattered among the nations (Mic. 5:7–8; Ezek. 5:10–12; 6:8; 12:15–16; 14:21–23; 17:21). Yet God's sovereign purpose was to bring them back (Mic. 2:12–13; 4:6–8), a chastened people who would be forgiven and cleansed (Mic. 7:18–20; Zeph. 3:11–13). God would carry them through the peril of exile (Isa. 46:3–4). In the end he would send some of the survivors to the nations in order to declare his glory to those who have not heard, and from these non-Israelites God would select priests and Levites (Isa. 66:19–21). Fugitives from the ends of the earth would turn to the Lord and be saved (Isa. 45:20–25; cf. Zech. 8:23; Joel 2:32; Zeph. 3:8–9)!

The New Covenant

Closely associated with the restoration of a remnant are the promises of a new covenant. Two prophets roughly contemporary with each other describe a new binding agreement which God would establish with the nations of Israel and Judah. The Lord instructed the first of these prophets, Jeremiah of Jerusalem, to record his visions about the nation's future hope (Jer. 30:2). While the majority of Jeremiah's oracles bleakly describe the death of the nation, the oracles in chapters 30–33 are largely optimistic. Though Jeremiah never retracted his predictions of disaster for his own generation, he held forth a distant hope for restoration that positively shone in contrast with the immediate anticipation of doom. He consistently maintained that the nation possessed a future, even though it was under the sentence of death, and more particularly, even

Figure 1.2

The Remnant Theology

◆ **The return of a remnant**
◆ **The new covenant**
  • **Forgiveness**
  • **David's kingship**
◆ **Gift of the Spirit**
◆ **Restoration of the land**
◆ **Day of salvation for the nations**

though the dynasty of David was being cut off at the roots. Hints of this future had been given previously (Jer. 3:14–18; 5:18; 16:14–15, 21; 23:3–8; 24:4–7; 27:21–22; 29:10–14), but in chapters 30–33 it is described in detail.

The central message of the optimistic oracles was that Yahweh intended to bring Israel back to her land (Jer. 30:3; 31:17; 33:7). The prophet vividly described the sufferings of exile, called the "time of trouble for Jacob" (Jer. 30:7). It would be a time of terror (Jer. 30:5) and pain (Jer. 30:6) when the ghostly figure of Rachel, the mother of the Benjamite tribe in the south and the grandmother of the Ephraimite tribe in the north, would weep for her banished children (Jer. 31:15). Yet this distress would come to an end, and the Israelites would be saved (Jer. 30:7b). The bondage of exile would be broken, and the nation once more would serve a king from David's line (Jer. 30:8–9). Though Yahweh would not allow the sinful nation to go unpunished (Jer. 30:11b; 33:1–5), its incurable wound would be healed (Jer. 30:12–15, 17; 33:6; cf. 8:22; 10:19). Though its ropes were broken (Jer. 10:20), Israel's fallen tent would be pitched again (Jer. 30:18). The nation would be saved from the land of exile (Jer. 30:10–11). The community would be revived, and its new leader would be deeply devoted to the Lord (Jer. 30:19–22).

Of course, such wonderful promises would be fulfilled for only a remnant (Jer. 31:7b), those who survived the sword of exile (Jer. 31:2). Jeremiah's purchase of the field owned by his cousin in Anathoth served as a sign pointing toward the predicted restoration (Jer. 32:1–15). The field of Anathoth, now owned by Jeremiah, represented all the fields which would be repossessed after the exile had ended (Jer. 32:43–44).

The promise of a new covenant is the theological climax of Jeremiah's consolation oracles. It was to be established with the survivors of a unified nation, that is, with both the houses of Israel and Judah (Jer. 31:31). The contrast between this new covenant and the Mosaic covenant is profound (Jer. 31:32). Whereas the Sinai covenant was spelled out in an external law code, the new covenant would be internally written in human hearts (Jer. 31:33). Whereas the Sinai covenant was grounded in a motif of reward for obedience and punishment for disobedience, the new covenant would be grounded in forgiveness (Jer. 31:34; 33:8). Whereas the justice of the old was by retribution, the justice of the new was by pardon (Jer. 32:36–41). And whereas the old could be ended by divine rejection of the nation for its sin, the new was guaranteed forever (Jer. 31:35–37; 32:40).

Associated with the new covenant that Yahweh promised was the revival of David's dynastic kingship. Jeremiah had prophesied elsewhere of the righteous Branch that would sprout from David's line (Jer. 23:5–6), and so had Isaiah a century earlier (Isa. 11:1; cf. 6:13b). This restoration was clearly to be associated with the return of the nation from exile (Jer. 23:3–4, 7–8; 33:6–13). The ancient promise that David would never lack a descendant to reign from his throne (2 Sam. 7:16; 23:5; Ps. 89:35–37) would thus be fulfilled (Jer. 33:17). Furthermore, the priests and Levites were guaranteed a perpetual ministry (Jer. 33:18). This covenant with David and the priests was bound by Yahweh's most solemn promise (Jer. 33:19–26).

The second prophet who spoke of a future covenant was Ezekiel. Though the kings of David's line had been abusive shepherds over the southern nation (Ezek. 34:1–10), and though the sheep of Judah had been scattered in exile (vv. 5–6), God determined to seek out his lost sheep. He would regather the exiles (Ezek. 36:24), cleanse them of their sins (Ezek. 36:25; 37:23), give to them a new heart (Ezek. 36:26; see also 11:19), and bestow upon them the Holy Spirit (Ezek. 36:27). He would restore them to their ancestral land and shepherd them with justice (Ezek. 36:28; 34:11–16). Over them he would place the best possible shepherd, a leader like David (Ezek. 34:23–24; 37:25). And for his regathered flock God would establish a covenant of peace so that they might live in safety in their land (Ezek. 34:25). Abundant rain, fertility, freedom, and security would be graciously provided to sustain them (Ezek. 34:26–31). This covenant of peace is almost certainly the same as what Jeremiah describes as a "new covenant."

There is little question but that the postexilic community, who returned from exile under the permission of Cyrus of Persia, expected the new covenant and all its ramifications to be fulfilled immediately. Certainly some statements by Jeremiah point in this direction (Jer. 23:3–8; 30:3, 10; 31:23–25; 50:4–5, 19–20). The disillusionment of the community when the new covenant was not fulfilled immediately is apparent in the postexilic works of Zechariah, Haggai, and Malachi. In the New Testament, of course, the new covenant is alluded to extensively (Matt. 26:28; Rom. 11:27; 1 Cor. 11:25; 2 Cor. 3:4–18; Heb. 8:7–13; 9:15; 12:24). The new covenant was established in the death and resurrection of Jesus Christ, and its benefits extend to all who come to faith in him.

The full scope and the proper interpretation of the new covenant are debated by various schools of theology. Covenant theologians believe that the predictions of Jeremiah and Ezekiel regarding Israel, Judah, the return from exile, the restoration of David's dynasty, and the rebuilding of Jerusalem and Zion are fulfilled in the post-Easter people of God. Older dispensational theologians argue that the only true fulfilment will come at the end of history in the millennial reign of Christ in Jerusalem with the Jews reestablished in their ancient land, the Zion temple rebuilt, and the Jewish priests practicing the ancient rituals. Newer dispensationalists modify this picture by conceding that there is a true fulfilment of the Davidic covenant in the present, though a future fulfilment will come as well. All Christian interpreters agree, however, that the establishment of the new covenant is anchored solidly in the passion of Jesus and that the implications of the new covenant stretch ahead into the eschatological future. The crucial point to be noted here is that with the establishment of the new covenant by Jesus' death on the cross, in some sense the last days began then!

The hope for a restored remnant, a new covenant, and all the attendant blessings of the last days is most fully expressed in the concept of salvation. Of course, the word "salvation" does multiple duty for victory in war, survival in the midst of disaster, and spiritual redemption, forgiveness, and restoration. This interplay of ideas figures strongly in the prophetic message, for in the days of fulfilment God will save his people from exile (Jer. 30:10; 31:7–9; 46:27; Zeph. 3:14–20; Zech. 8:7; 10:6), from destruction (Jer. 30:11; 46:28; Zech. 9:14–16), from abuse (Ezek. 34:22), and from their sins (Ezek. 36:29; 37:23). Without doubt the most exalted language of salvation is found in the latter chapters of Isaiah, where God describes himself as Israel's Savior (Isa. 43:3, 11–12; 45:15–17, 21; 49:24–26; 52:7–10; 56:1; 59:15b–17; 60:16–18; 62:1; 63:1, 5) and Redeemer (Isa. 41:14; 43:14; 44:6, 24; 47:4; 48:17; 49:7, 26; 54:5, 8; 59:20; 60:16; 63:16). When the remnant returns from exile, it will be the "day of salvation" (Isa. 49:8–13). And the Lord will save not only Israel, but also the nations (Isa. 42:4; 49:6; 51:4–6, 8b; 52:10, 15).

The Messianic Hope

We have come a considerable distance in our attempt to grasp the message of the Old Testament prophets concerning the last days. They anticipated the last days as a time of judgment and salvation. We know, of course, that a judgment in history was accomplished in the exile. We also know that those who returned from exile did not exhaust the prediction of salvation and victory. To the contrary, they met with deep disappointment. Still, the hope for the future remained firm. God would restore a remnant, he would establish a new covenant of forgiveness, and he would raise up in David's line a new king. Salvation was on the way, even if it had not yet fully arrived! Now we are ready to explore how this salvation would come in the last days.

Central to the oracles of hope in the Hebrew prophets is a messianic figure who would appear in the last days. The future promises of the day of Yahweh, the last days, the restoration of the remnant, the establishment of the new covenant, and the double-edged visions of judgment and salvation all looked to someone who was coming. Of course, the title *māšîaḥ* ("Messiah, anointed one") was used of various figures, including priests (Lev. 4:3), kings (1 Sam. 16:6; 24:6; Ps. 2:2), patriarchs (Ps. 105:15), and even a heathen potentate whom God wished to use to achieve his purposes in history (Isa. 45:1). Nevertheless, the hope for the future included an individual par excellence, a messianic figure anointed by Yahweh and endowed with special powers.

To be sure, this messianic figure was described under a variety of rubrics other than the title "Messiah." Furthermore, it is not always clear that these different descriptions are referring to the same person. It would remain for Jesus and the apostles to bring together the prophecies into a single stream. Nevertheless, that a future leader is in view is unmistakable even apart from the New Testament. The vision for this future leader generally falls into two categories, the image of a king and the image of a servant.

The Davidic Messiah

The first image is royal. That the word *māšîaḥ* has royal connotations is evident in the designation of the kings of Israel as the anointed of Yahweh (Ps. 18:50; 132:10, 17). Yahweh, the God enthroned in the heavens, had also enthroned his "Anointed One" on Mount Zion (Ps. 2:1–6). Thus, with the demise of David's dynasty by exile, it is no surprise to find the prophets looking ahead to the last days when once again a royal figure from David's line would rule Israel (Amos 9:11–12). This coming one, born to be a king, would reign on David's throne forever (Isa. 9:6–7). He would arise as a shoot from Jesse's stump (Isa. 11:1), and he would assemble the exiles of Israel from among the nations (Isa. 11:10–16; Hos. 3:4–5). His throne would be established in love, and his administration would be carried out in justice and righteousness (Isa. 16:4b–5; 32:1; Jer. 23:5–6; 30:8–9; 33:14–26).

The imagery of a coming king overlaps the imagery of a coming shepherd, for kingship in ancient Israel was viewed as a type of shepherding (Ezek. 34:22–24; Mic. 5:2–5; see also Ps. 78:70–72). Just as the images of king and shepherd overlap, so also do the images of king and son of God. The king from David's dynasty was adopted as God's royal son upon his ascension to the throne (Ps. 2:7; 72:1; 89:26–27; 2 Sam. 7:14). Yet another title converges in this anticipation, Daniel's prediction of one coming "like a son of man" (Dan. 7:13–14). Daniel's vision heralds the coming one as a heavenly figure to whom would be given everlasting sovereignty over all the nations of the earth.

It is probable that in the postexilic community there were hopes that these glowing promises would be fulfilled in Zerubbabel. After all, Zerubbabel was a descendant of David (1 Chron. 3:19), he was a leader of the postexilic community (Ezra 2:1–2; Neh. 7:6–7; 12:1, 47; Hag. 2:2), he supervised the rebuilding of the great altar (Ezra 3:1–6), and he laid the foundation for the second temple (Ezra 3:8–11). Assisted by Joshua the high priest and spurred on by the prophets Haggai and Zechariah (Ezra 5:1–2; 6:14–15; Hag. 1:1–2, 12–15; 2:1–5; Zech. 4:6–7), he completed the temple (Ezra 6:14–15; Zech. 4:8–10a). He, along with Joshua the high priest, was declared to be the anointed of the Lord (Zech. 4:12–14).

Nevertheless, Zerubbabel for all his credentials only foreshadowed the coming one. In Haggai's final oracle Yahweh declared that the entire universe would one day be shaken (Hag. 2:21; cf. 2:6–7). The potentates of foreign nations would be overthrown, and their armies would be turned against each other (Hag. 2:22). On the day of this apocalyptic climax God would establish Zerubbabel as his chosen executive (Hag. 2:23). This favored status was expressed in the metaphor of a signet ring, the ring engraved with the king's seal that was used to endorse all official documents. Earlier Jeremiah had used the same metaphor in his judgment against Jehoiachin (Jer. 22:24). Jehoiachin, Zerubbabel's grandfather, had been removed as God's signet ring. Now the judgment would be reversed.

The fact that Zerubbabel died without seeing this great honor bestowed upon him raises the question of a failed prophecy. Was the prophecy to be taken literally, and if so, why was it not fulfilled? Was it conditional on Israel's response?[2] Would it be fulfilled by Zerubbabel resurrected from the dead? Or was the promise more on the order of the prediction about the coming of Elijah (Mal. 4:5–6), which, according to Jesus, was fulfilled by John the Baptist (Matt. 17:10–13; see also Luke 1:16–17)? Would someone else, a Zerubbabel-like figure, arise to fulfil the prediction? Was the promise messianic, and was it fulfilled by Jesus of Nazareth, as many older interpreters have thought inasmuch as Zerubbabel was in the messianic lineage (Matt. 1:12)? Is there yet an eschatological fulfilment to be accomplished at the end of the age (see Zech. 4:2–14; Rev. 11:3–4)? It seems likely that Zerubbabel serves as a typological link between the promise and the coming Messiah,[3] a link reinforced by Zechariah's preaching (see, e.g., Zech. 6:9–15).

Joshua and his fellow priests were symbols of a blessing still to come, the blessing of the advent of God's servant, the Branch (Zech. 3:8). With the advent of the Branch, the sins of the land would be removed in a single day (Zech. 3:9b). This Branch, described as Zerubbabel, would build the temple of Yahweh (Zech. 6:12). Yet the promises associated with him are much greater than anything that ever attended the work of postexilic Zerubbabel, for the Branch was destined to sit on his throne and rule in majesty, and there would be a harmonization between priestly and royal leadership (Zech. 6:13). People would come from faraway lands to help build Yahweh's temple (Zech. 6:15), a prediction that could hardly refer to the building of the second temple. Once again, the prophecy seems to be a double entendre. In a near sense, it refers to the building of the second temple, but in an eschatological sense, it stretches ahead to a future era.

Later, of course, the Book of Zechariah looks directly to a glorious future when Jerusalem's king will come riding on a donkey (Zech. 9:9). This king would proclaim peace to the nations (Zech. 9:10). Although the return from exile was already completed, the prediction was not exhausted that God would gather his scattered exiles. There was still a regathering to be anticipated (Zech. 10:6–12).

The final two oracles of Zechariah are filled with the images of war and victory (Zech. 9–11, 12–14). Among these oracles is the prediction that upon the survivors of Jerusalem would be poured out a spirit of grace and prayer. This spirit, in turn, would produce great mourning for one who had been pierced (Zech. 12:10). Though there are some translational issues in fixing the identity of the pierced one, John certainly understood that the prediction ultimately pointed to Christ (John 19:37). Because of the pierced one a cleansing fountain for purification, a beautiful metaphor for forgiveness, would be opened to all Jerusalem (Zech. 13:1).

Yet another remarkable prediction anticipated the striking down of the shepherd-king. The sword of execution would be called forth, the shepherd close to Yahweh's side would be smitten, and the sheep would be scattered with only a third surviving as a remnant (Zech. 13:7–9). In a final vision of war and victory, Zechariah depicted Yahweh as the consummate warrior who would defend Jerusalem with all his angelic hosts (Zech. 14:1–5). In the end he would reign as king over the whole earth

(Zech. 14:9), and all the nations would come to Jerusalem to worship him (Zech. 14:16–19).

These final two oracles of Zechariah raise significant eschatological questions. The historical approach attempts to locate their fulfilment in the postexilic period, usually in the intertestamental period. Thus the war in 9:1–8 is sometimes taken to describe Alexander the Great's invasion of Palestine, while the war in 9:11–10:1 is taken to be fulfilled, or at least partially fulfilled, in the Maccabean conflict with the Seleucids in the second century B.C. A thoroughgoing futuristic approach, on the other hand, relegates all of the wars to the close of the age. A spiritual interpretation might attempt to treat the wars as symbols of the spread of the Christian gospel in an antagonistic world.

Each of these positions has strengths and weaknesses. Certain historical parallels between the predictions in Zechariah and the wars of the intertestamental period do in fact exist. However, the conversion of the Philistines certainly never happened (Zech. 9:6–7; cf. 1 Macc. 3:41)! Furthermore, the temple was not protected: it was violated in 167 B.C. by Antiochus Epiphanes and destroyed in A.D. 70 by Titus. The Israelites, far from being restored and established forever, were overrun by both the Greeks and the Romans.

To relegate everything in Zechariah's oracles to the end of the world is not entirely satisfactory either, for although the wars themselves might parallel, to some degree, the apocalyptic visions of John, various problems remain. The Philistines, for instance, have long since disappeared. The references to the dispersion of Israelites in Assyria and Egypt seem to be obvious references to the Old Testament exile, not some modern situation. Furthermore, the New Testament regards some associated predictions, particularly those about the coming of the new king, as being fulfilled in the first advent of Christ.

The spiritual interpretation is even more tenuous, since it resorts to massive allegorization of details with little rationale for doing so. Since none of the approaches is fully satisfactory, it is appropriate to refrain from dogmatism. It should be pointed out, however, that the final oracles in Zechariah exhibit the general characteristics of prophetic-apocalyptic literature. This means that in addition to the extensive use of symbolism the writer superimposes images of the end of the age over allusions to contemporary or intermediate events. Above all, prophetic-apocalyptic literature seeks to assure the readers that the victory of God and his people is certain. It must be remembered that this approach does not produce a systematic and consistent eschatological outline. It does not move from point A to point B to point C in logical fashion. Rather, the genre's basic aim is to convey an intense belief in God's divine intervention before the end so as to accomplish his redemptive purposes. It does so through a host of images, all of which may not be immediately clear. Indeed, some of them may become clear only as one sees what God's future brings.

The Servant-Messiah

The second messianic image associated with the last days is described in the later chapters of Isaiah. The figure of the ʿEbed-Yahweh ("the servant of the Lord") is used with striking fluidity to refer to many and to one. Collectively, the servant of the Lord is Israel, the remnant of the nation which went into exile (Isa. 41:8; 44:1–2, 21; 45:4; 48:20; 49:3). Individually, the servant of the Lord represents a figure who would bring justice to the nations (Isa. 42:1–4), one who would reconcile Israel to God (Isa. 49:5) and bring salvation to the Gentiles at the ends of the earth (Isa. 49:6). He would be a figure of vicarious suffering and rejection (Isa. 49:7; 52:13–53:12).

The most intriguing question about the figure of the servant is identity. Who is the servant? As the metaphor is developed, it seems to fluctuate between a collective figure for the nation Israel and an individual figure who has a mission to Israel as well as to the world. Even in biblical times this question was vexing, for the Ethiopian proselyte struggled with it, as is evident in his query, "Who is the prophet talking about, himself or someone else?" (Acts 8:34). As a collective figure, the metaphor clearly represents the nation Israel, but this identification hardly exhausts the metaphor. It is when the metaphor depicts an individual that it is most intriguing. Could the individual servant be the prophet himself? Is he a king of David's line yet to come? Could he be a historical figure like the suffering prophet Jeremiah?

Yahweh himself introduces his servant as one who has been chosen and endowed with the Holy Spirit to bring justice to the nations (Isa. 42:1). This servant stands in sharp contrast to Cyrus the Persian, who was also God's instrument (Isa. 44:28; 45:1, 13). Cyrus would serve Yahweh's purpose unwittingly, but the servant of the Lord would accomplish Yahweh's purpose intentionally and faithfully. Unlike the mighty Cyrus, this servant would not come with violence and noise (Isa. 42:2–3). He would not crush the weak. Rather, he would come with patient obedience and dogged persistence, pressing on until he had established justice for the nations (Isa. 42:4).

In one sense, the call for the servant to establish a universal justice must refer to the purpose of God for Israel. Abraham, the ancestor of the nation, had been promised that all the nations would be blessed through his offspring (Gen. 12:1–3). The Israelites had been called to serve as priests for the nations of the world (Exod. 19:3–6), though this calling was conditional upon Israel's faithfulness to the covenant. Because of repeated covenant breaking, the ideal had never been realized, though hints of it are to be found in the books of Ruth and Jonah. Now, however, the ideal is revived in the first of the Servant Songs.[4] Though God's collective servant had failed, his individual servant would succeed. God's original purpose had not changed. He was interested in the nations, and he had chosen his individual servant to fulfil his great mission (Isa. 42:5–17). This time the mission would be accomplished!

Then comes the explanation of Israel's failure in the servant's role. All along she had been deaf and blind to God's greater purpose (Isa. 42:18–19). She had seen, yet she had not seen (Isa. 42:20). Though she had been given the law at Sinai (Isa. 42:21), she had fallen prey to the Deuteronomic curse because of her continual covenant breaking (Isa. 42:22). Yahweh had handed her over to her enemies because of her disobedience (Isa. 42:23–24). She went through the holocaust of exile, yet even in this distress she did not understand nor take to heart what had happened (Isa. 42:25).

The coming individual servant, however, would be truly effective in turning the wayward servant, Israel, back to God. This was Yahweh's promise. Though the coming servant would be despised and abhorred (Isa. 49:7a), in the end he would be honored by the nations because Yahweh had chosen him (Isa. 49:7b).[5] As Yahweh's servant he would call for salvation, and Yahweh would answer (Isa. 49:8a). Paul interprets this redemptive mission of the servant as the time of God's favor to the nations (2 Cor. 6:2). Those in captivity would hear the cry of freedom, "Come out" (Isa. 49:9a). People from the ends of the earth[6] would come to share in this redemptive benefit (Isa. 49:11–13).

The individual servant stands in sharpest contrast to the collective servant Israel. Whereas Israel is blind, deaf (Isa. 42:19), and unresponsive (Isa. 50:2), the individual will be receptive in his attitude toward Yahweh and obedient in his actions (Isa. 50:4–5). Whereas Israel is stubborn, with a neck of iron and a forehead of bronze (Isa. 48:4), the coming servant will not hesitate to fulfil God's purpose for him (Isa. 50:5b). Furthermore, this coming servant will suffer greatly. He will be beaten and abused (Isa. 49:7; 50:6). Nevertheless, his end will be glory not disgrace. His determination will be unflagging, and God will vindicate him at last (Isa. 50:7–9).

Now follows what has become for many the single most important passage about the individual servant. The prophet has held up for examination and shame the failed mission of the collective servant. He has also anticipated the fully successful mission of the perfect servant who is yet to come. Nevertheless, in spite of his ultimate success, the perfect servant will also be a figure of terrible suffering, which the prophet describes in detail.

In public opinion the coming servant will seem to fail. He will arouse both admiration and horror (Isa. 52:13–14). His work will be a priestly work (Isa. 52:15a),[7] causing mute wonder and amazement on the part of the nations and potentates of the world (Isa. 52:15b). His mission will be so unusual that it will strain credulity in all who see him (Isa. 53:1), not the least of whom will be the Jewish people themselves (John 12:37–38; Rom. 10:16). His beauty will be in his gentle character, not his outward appearance (Isa. 53:2–3). He will suffer greatly, empathizing so fully with the sorrow of the people that he will suffer vicariously for their sins (Isa. 53:4–6). Still, in spite of torture and abuse, he will not retaliate (Isa. 53:7). Above all, he will suffer innocently and quietly (Isa. 53:8–9; 1 Peter 2:22–23). After he dies, he will be given a grave with the wicked and the rich (Isa. 53:9; Matt. 27:57–60).

Was this innocent, vicarious suffering to be permitted by a holy God? Most certainly! In fact, it was precisely the will of God that this suffering should be accomplished (Isa. 53:10a), because in it God would effect a sacrificial expiation (Isa. 53:10b). Though the servant would be cut off without descendants (Isa. 53:8b), yet, paradoxically, God would preserve for him posterity (Isa. 53:10c). Though he would die a horrible death (Isa. 53:8c), God would grant him prolonged life (Isa. 53:10c). When the ordeal was over, vindication, victory, and justification would be the result (Isa. 53:11–12).

The Prophetic Vision of the Last Days

It is well to summarize where we have been in this survey of Israel's prophetic hope in order to better appreciate what the New Testament writers inherited from their past. By now it should be apparent that in the Hebrew prophets the vision of the last days was a matrix of events and figures superimposed on each other. The vision was often couched in double entendres concerning the near future as well as the indeterminate future. It included both judgment and salvation. On the one hand, the day of Yahweh involved the exile of the two nations in the eighth and sixth centuries as a judgment in history based on the Deuteronomic code. On the other hand, the same rubric anticipated the arraignment of the nations of the whole earth before the court of almighty God. Yet images of salvation are also readily apparent. The God who would send his people away into exile would also reclaim them from their dispersion. A remnant would survive, and with them God would establish a new covenant, forgiving their sins and giving back their land. The two nations would be reunited into a single commonwealth. There would be perpetual prosperity, while Jerusalem would become the capital of the world. This hope was not for Israel alone. A remnant from among the nations also would look to the Lord and be saved. Gentiles, once completely estranged from the commonwealth of Israel, would be joined to the holy community of God's people. Finally, the gift of the Spirit would be poured out upon all people, both Israel and the nations.

Associated with these wonderful predictions about the future was the messianic hope. While the primary images of a royal figure and a servant figure are not interchangeable, the raw data within the oracles of the prophets made possible the convergence of the two. To be sure, the Jews of Jesus' day saw the figure of the servant only in terms of their own nation. Jesus was the first to give it a messianic interpretation. In a preliminary sense, Cyrus of Persia was a messiah for God's people. However, Cyrus hardly measured up to the majestic vision of the servant of

Figure 1.3

The Prophets' Vision
of the Last Days
(DAY OF YHWH)

◆ Judgment of the nations
◆ Salvation of God's people
◆ Union of Israel and Judah
◆ Regathering of the exiles
◆Restoration of a remnant
◆ Addition of Gentiles to the
   commonwealth of Israel
◆Pouring out of the gift of
   the Spirit
◆ Coming of the royal figure
   (Messiah)
◆ Coming of the suffering
   servant
◆ The new covenant
◆ Jerusalem the capital of the
   world

the Lord to whom all the nations of the world would come for salvation. Zerubbabel and Joshua, the royal and priestly leaders of the postexilic community, were also partial fulfilments. In a larger sense they served as signs pointing beyond themselves to the future.

The restoration for which the repatriates hoped was meager. Dogged by a series of crop failures, obstinate neighbors, and flagging spirits, the postexilic community struggled to complete the second temple. When their work was finally done, the glory of the Lord did not flood this sanctuary as it had the first one, nor did Ezekiel's glorious vision of a new commonwealth materialize. Accordingly, the hope for full restoration was pushed ahead by the postexilic prophets into the unknown future. The final note of the Hebrew prophets pointed to a future day when Yahweh's messenger would come to the temple on Zion (Mal. 3:1–4). How would this future materialize? When would the last days come? The Hebrew Bible ends on an unfinished note. The hope of the exiles was deferred to the future.

The Jewish nation never completely recovered from the exile. Archaeological data indicate that many survivors from the northern nation were absorbed into the southern nation in the late eighth century B.C. The colonists the Assyrians moved into the land of Palestine to replace the expatriates intermarried with the Israelites who were left (2 Kings 17:24–41). Those who went into exile from the northern nation disappeared for all practical purposes. In addition, many of the exiles from Judah chose not to return to Palestine. Though a remnant did return, they never entirely escaped the domination of the empire builders. Except for a century of independence following the Maccabean revolt, they were the victims of the Babylonians, the Persians, the Greeks, and the Romans. Finally, in the late first and early second centuries A.D., they were dispersed for good by the Romans.

For most of Israel, then, a tradition had to be fashioned that could function in a world without the Davidic monarchy, the temple, the priesthood, Mount Zion, and the homeland. This tradition, called Judaism, replaced the temple with the synagogue, the daily sacrifice with prayer, and the altar with the family table. The Jewish home acquired the centrality that Zion once held. After the destruction of Herod's temple by the Romans in A.D. 70, all Jews, even Palestinian ones, were forced to accept this shift in tradition.

The Christians, however, had a different perspective. They did not view the wonderful promises of the Hebrew prophets as a failed hope. Rather, the time of fulfilment had actually dawned with the events surrounding the birth of Jesus of Nazareth. In the faith of the New Testament, the emphasis shifts from Sinai and Zion, Moses and David, toward the person of Jesus Christ. To be precise, Sinai and Zion were not so much rejected as they were fulfilled and completed in Jesus.

The Dawn of the Time of Fulfilment

Without question, the New Testament writers concluded that the last days began with the Jesus event. This conclusion is explicitly stated by several authors, and it is implicit in nearly every document in the New Testament. "In the past God spoke to our forefathers through the prophets at many times and in various ways, but in these last days he has spoken to us by his Son," begins the author of Hebrews. F. F. Bruce is surely correct when he says that by the phrase "the last days" the author means much more than just "recently." Rather, it is "a literal rendering of the Hebrew phrase which is used in the Old Testament to denote the epoch when the words of the prophets will be fulfilled."[8] At Pentecost Peter gave a similar interpretation of the gift of the Spirit: "This is what was spoken by the prophet Joel: 'In the last days, God says, I will pour out my Spirit on all people'" (Acts 2:16–17a). If the Spirit had come, then the last days had begun. Later, in his first epistle, Peter says that Christ was "chosen before the creation of the world, but was revealed in these last times for your sake" (1 Peter 1:20). Thus the last times, the days of fulfilment, had arrived. John can frankly say, "Dear children, this is the last hour . . ." (1 John 2:18a). The rise of many false messiahs was proof: "This is how we know it is the last hour" (1 John 2:18b). Paul could speak as though he lived on the very brink of the end: "Our salvation is nearer now than when we first believed. The night is nearly over; the day is almost here" (Rom. 13:11b–12a); and "The God of peace will soon crush Satan under your feet" (Rom. 16:20). Again and again the nearness of the consummation is urged in statements like "The Lord is near" (Phil. 4:5), "The end of all things is near" (1 Peter 4:7a), "The time is short" (1 Cor. 7:29a), "This world in its present form is passing away" (1 Cor. 7:31b), and "The Lord's coming is near. . . . The Judge is standing at the door!" (James 5:8–9). God's final salvation is "ready to be revealed in the last time" (1 Peter 1:5). Clearly the earliest Christians believed that they were living in the last days.

The Evidence of the Birth Narratives

The roots of the idea that the last days began with the Jesus event are to be found in the birth narratives of the Gospels. In the third Gospel, Luke introduces an important and recurring expression—"filled with the Spirit." The significance of this phrase is best understood against the background of the synagogue teaching that the prophetic sequence of inspired speech had broken off with the last of the writing prophets. Similarly, intertestamental writings note that "prophets [had] ceased to appear" (1 Macc. 9:27; see also 4:46; 14:41). It was believed that in the days of the Messiah the Spirit of the Lord would become active again, for the quenched Spirit would return.[9] By stressing the activity of the Spirit, Luke calls attention to the fact that the messianic era had begun. Elizabeth (Luke 1:41), Zechariah (Luke 1:67), Mary (Luke 1:35), Simeon (Luke 2:26–27), and Jesus (Luke 4:1, 18) were all filled with or moved by the Spirit. The prophets had said that the messianic age would be characterized by the gift of the Spirit, and the Spirit was now active! Significantly, in his history of the early church Luke continued to record the outpouring of the Spirit upon the first Christians (Acts 2:4; 4:8, 31; 6:3, 5; 7:55; 9:17; 11:24; 13:9, 52).

Along other lines, the birth of John the Baptist was a fulfilment of Malachi's prophecy of the coming of Elijah. Ministering in "the spirit and power of Elijah," this coming figure would, as Malachi said, "turn the hearts of the fathers to their children" (Luke 1:17; cf. Mal. 4:6). Of course, John denied being Elijah literally (John 1:21), but Jesus indicated that John had fulfilled the prediction of the coming of Elijah before the day of Yahweh (Matt. 17:10–13).

As the birth narratives progress, it becomes increasingly clear that Matthew and Luke intend their readers to understand the prophetic hope of Israel to be fulfilled in Jesus of Nazareth. The parallelisms between Nathan's prophetic oracle about David's son and the angel's annunciation to Mary are especially striking (2 Sam. 7:9, 13–14, 16; Luke 1:32–33). Nathan had said the name of David's son would be made great; Gabriel announced that Jesus would be great. Nathan had said that the throne of David's son would be established; Gabriel said that God would give Jesus the throne of his father David. Nathan had said David's son would be called God's son; Gabriel said Jesus would be called the Son of the Most High. Nathan had said the kingdom of David's son would endure perpetually; Gabriel said Jesus would reign over the house of Jacob forever, and his kingdom would never end.

Moreover, the titles given to Jesus in the birth narratives are emphatic declarations that he was the coming one: "Son of God" (Luke 1:32, 35), "Lord" (Luke 1:43; 2:11), "Savior" (Luke 2:11), "Messiah" (Luke 2:11, 26; Matt. 1:1, 17–18; 2:4), "Immanuel" (Matt. 1:23), "King" (Matt. 2:2), "Shepherd" (Matt. 2:6), and "son of David" (Matt. 1:1; Luke 2:4). In addition, in both the Magnificat of Mary and the Song of Zechariah the language of fulfilment is explicit. The day of Yahweh, when all the proud and lofty would be humbled (cf. Isa. 2:12), had dawned with the birth of Jesus (Luke 1:51–52). This was the time of fulfilment to Israel, God's servant (Luke 1:54–55). This was the day of the Savior in the house of David as the prophets had foretold (Luke 1:69). This was the promised time of forgiveness (Luke 1:77). This was the dawn of the rising sun that would shine on those living in the shadow of death (Isa. 9:2; 42:7; 58:8; 60:1–2; Mal. 4:2; Luke 1:78–79). The birth of Jesus, according to Simeon's Spirit-inspired prayer, brought salvation for "all people, a light for revelation to the Gentiles and for glory to your people Israel" (Luke 2:31b–32). Anna, Simeon's counterpart in the temple, heralded the coming of Jesus as the fulfilment of the promise that Jerusalem would be redeemed (Luke 2:38). In the annunciation to Joseph, Jesus was lauded as the one who would save Israel from their sins (Matt. 1:21). And according to Matthew's recapitulation of events, Jesus' birth fulfilled the word of the Lord given to Isaiah about the Immanuel child (Matt. 1:22–23; Isa. 7:10–17).

The Fulfilment Motif in the Gospels

Wave after wave of fulfilment passages dots the four Gospels. While Mark and John do not have birth narratives, they are no less emphatic that the Jesus event was the inauguration of the time of fulfilment. Mark's Gospel begins with the majestic announcement, "The beginning of the gospel about Jesus Messiah, the Son of God!" "The time has come!" Jesus preached. "The kingdom of God is near. Repent and believe the good news!" (Mark 1:15). "The true light that gives light to every man was coming into the world," writes John (John 1:9). Though the glory of God had not returned to fill the second temple as it had the first one, there is no doubt that for John it finally made its appearance in the birth of God's Son: "We have seen his glory," he wrote, for "the Word became flesh and lived for a while among us" (John 1:14). Repeatedly in the fourth Gospel Jesus notes that some expectation has been fulfilled: "A time is coming and has now come when . . ." (John 4:23; 5:25; 16:32). And at Nazareth he boldly declared that he was the one anointed to proclaim the year of God's favor (Isa. 61:1–2): "Today this scripture is fulfilled in your hearing" (Luke 4:16–21).

MATTHEW

In their portraits of Jesus the Evangelists demonstrated both explicitly and implicitly that Jesus was the coming one and that the messianic age had begun. By striking parallelisms which could hardly have been missed by his Jewish readers Matthew shows that Jesus embodied Israel. He went down into Egypt to avoid destruction (Matt. 2:13; cf. Gen. 45:4–8) and was brought up again as God's Son (Matt. 2:15; cf. Exod. 4:22–23; Hos. 11:1). He passed through the waters (Matt. 3:13–17; cf. Exod. 14:22) and was tempted in the desert (Matt. 4:1–11; cf. Deut. 8:3). Whereas Moses ascended Sinai to receive the law, Jesus sat on the mountain to give God's authoritative interpretation of the law (Matt. 5:1–2, 17, 21–22, 27–28, 31–32, 33–34, 38–39, 43–44; cf. Exod. 20:1–17). The new and greater Moses was transfigured just as the original Moses (Matt. 17:1–3; cf. Exod. 34:29–35). And it was no accident that in his triumphant entry into Jerusalem Jesus was hailed as the new king who would ascend to Zion (Matt. 21:1–5; cf. Zech. 9:9–10). Though he was the stone rejected by the builders, he was destined to be the capstone (Matt. 21:42; cf. Ps. 118:22–23). In his death he suffered the dereliction of exile (Matt. 27:45–46), but on Easter morning he triumphed over his enemies in resurrection (Matt. 28:1–10). The temple, the old center of faith on Zion, would soon be thrown down (Matt. 24:1–2), but the new center of faith would be Jesus, the Messiah, God's Son (Matt. 16:13–18).

MARK

Each Gospel in its own way describes Jesus as the fulfilment of the messianic hope. Mark's Gospel shows that until after the events of his passion and Easter Jesus was very careful about claiming messianic fulfilment. When evil spirits recognized him as the Holy One of God, he commanded them to silence regarding his identity (Mark 1:25, 34; 3:11–12). When he performed healings, he counseled those he healed not to tell anyone (Mark 1:44; 5:43; 7:36; 8:25–26). In fact, after his transfiguration he instructed his disciples not to tell anyone until after his resurrection (Mark 9:9–10). This so-called messianic secret is intelligible against the background of various popular messianic concepts that were current in Judaism, none of which corresponded in nature to Jesus' self-identification as the Messiah. So, to avoid misunderstanding, Jesus was careful in making messianic claims or inferences. However, as Mark's Gospel makes clear, this in no way detracted from the belief that Jesus was indeed the Messiah who was promised. His messiahship was of a higher order than were the popular concepts of messiahship, for he was the Son of God, a truth to which Mark calls attention again and again (Mark 1:1, 11; 3:11; 5:6–7; 9:7; 12:6–7; 13:32; 14:61–62). At the climax of the Gospel is the Roman executioner's exclamation, "Surely this man was the Son of God!" (Mark 15:39).

LUKE

Luke's Gospel, while similar to Mark and Matthew, still is distinctive for the number of times it describes people as being amazed at what they saw (Luke 1:12, 21, 63, 65; 2:9, 18, 33, 47–48; 4:22, 32, 36; 5:9, 26; 7:16; 8:25, 35, 37, 56; 9:34, 43, 45; 11:14, 38; 20:26; 24:4, 12, 22, 41). Their amazement compelled the question "Who is Jesus?" Luke's answer, of course, is that he is God's Son, the Messiah, who in his suffering and resurrection fulfilled what the Hebrew prophets had predicted (Luke 24:44–47). His advent in the world signaled the inauguration of the kingdom of God (Luke 4:43; 6:20; 8:1, 10; 9:2, 11, 60; 10:9–11; 12:32; 16:16; 17:20–21; 18:16–17, 24–25; 22:29). The fact that he exercised power over the demonic world meant that the kingdom of God had come (Luke 11:20).

In a travelogue section largely missing from the other Gospels, Luke demonstrates that Jesus was the prophet like Moses (see Deut. 18:18–19). From 9:51 through 19:44 Luke depicts Jesus en route to Jerusalem for his passion. This lengthy journey was not direct. Jesus began by heading south from Galilee through Samaria (Luke 9:52), visited Bethany near Jerusalem (Luke 10:38), later traveled on the northern border of Samaria (Luke 17:11), and then arrived in Jericho (Luke 18:35). Nevertheless, whether Jesus was headed north, south, east, or west, the ultimate goal was Jerusalem (Luke 9:51–53, 57; 10:1, 38; 13:22, 31–32; 17:11; 18:31, 35; 19:1, 28, 41).

Why did Luke go to such extraordinary literary measures to depict Jesus on this long journey south, a trip that normally should have taken only three days? Some scholars suggest that he wished to demonstrate that just as Moses traveled with the ancient twelve tribes through the wilderness on the way to the Promised Land, a journey during which he taught them and disciplined them in that "vast and dreadful desert" (Deut. 8:15), so Jesus led his twelve apostles on a new exodus toward its consummation in the new covenant and the kingdom of God.[10] Only Luke records Jesus' describing what would happen in Jerusalem as his "exodus," and it is almost certain that the use of this Greek word is deliberate (Luke 9:31). Certainly Jesus reminded the Twelve that the journey to Jerusalem would culminate in the fulfilment of the Old Testament predictions about the Son of man. He would be rejected, killed, and on the third day resurrected (Luke 18:31–34; see also 9:22, 44–45; 12:50; 13:33; 17:25). In a larger sense, the death of the nation in exile had its counterpart in the death of Jesus—and the hope of restoration had its counterpart in Jesus' resurrection.

For Luke, the entire complex of events in the life and death of Jesus was the culmination toward which the prophets pointed. His Gospel begins by speaking of "the things that have been fulfilled among us" (Luke 1:1). The appearance of Moses and Elijah at the transfiguration reinforces this idea (Luke 9:30–31). The conclusion of the Gospel narrates how Jesus opened the meaning of the Scriptures, explaining that Moses and all the prophets were speaking of him (Luke 24:27, 32, 44–47). If it is true that Moses and all the prophets speak of Jesus, then the prophetic oracles which predicted the coming exile of Israel and God's judgment upon the nations must have been typological of the Jesus event. The death of the nation and the promise of restoration were themes recapitulated in the story of Jesus.

John

The fourth Gospel also addresses the question "Who is Jesus?" John clearly states that his purpose in writing was that his readers might "believe that Jesus is the Messiah, the Son of God" (John 20:31). The frequent polemics between Jesus and the Jews in the fourth Gospel sharpen the issue, for in these dialogues John consciously seeks to demonstrate that only by faith in Jesus can men and women remain in continuity with the promises of the Hebrew Scriptures. The prophets had predicted the coming of a king; Jesus was that king (John 1:49). The Old Testament taught that Messiah was coming; he had now come (John 4:25–26)! Jesus' allusions to his coming death and resurrection in Jerusalem were grounded in the hope of the Hebrew Scriptures (John 2:22). He was the one whom the Scriptures had foretold (John 5:39–40). What once was anticipated as future had now arrived (John 4:21–23). While the crowds might debate the question of messiahship (John 7:25–44), Jesus plainly claimed to be the one for whom Abraham looked (John 8:56), and the one of whom Moses and the prophets wrote (John 1:45; 5:46–47). Even the doubts of those who disclaimed Jesus fulfilled the predictions of the prophets (John 12:37–41; Isa. 53:1; 6:10). And whereas the Hebrew prophets had also looked to a time of judgment in the last days, Jesus announced that the Father had assigned all judgment to him (John 5:22, 27, 30). Furthermore, Jesus declared his death on the cross to be "the time for judgment on this world." The prince of the world would be driven out (John 12:31; 16:8–11). Jesus' final words on the cross were uttered in the knowledge "that all was now completed . . . that the Scripture would be fulfilled" (John 19:28).

The New Covenant

Perhaps the most cogent sign confirming the dawn of the time of fulfilment lay in Jesus' remarks relating his death to the establishment of the new covenant anticipated by Jeremiah and Ezekiel. This new covenant, which was part of the matrix of events predicted for the last days, was central to the eucharistic words of Jesus at the Last Supper. On the night he was betrayed Jesus told the Twelve that the broken bread and cup of wine, while pointing to his imminent death, were also symbols of the inauguration of the new covenant of forgiveness (Matt. 26:28; Mark 14:24; Luke 22:20; 1 Cor. 11:25). The apostles were firmly convinced that the new covenant had been established by Jesus in his death (2 Cor. 3:6; Heb. 8:7–13; 9:15; 12:24). The promises had been fulfilled!

The Servant of the Lord

By the time the apostles began to preach, the motif of fulfilment had crystalized into a dominant theme. In the upper room Jesus had identified himself as the servant who would be numbered with the transgressors (Luke 22:37; cf. Isa. 53:12); his disciples understood this meaning clearly. Accordingly, Peter boldly declared from Solomon's Porch at the temple that "the God of our fathers has glorified his servant Jesus!" (Acts 3:13). God has now "raised up his servant" (Acts 3:26), just as he had promised. The death of Jesus was a fulfilment of Isaiah's theme of the suffering servant. "This is how God fulfilled what he had foretold through all the prophets" (Acts 3:18); in fact, "all the prophets from Samuel on, as many as have spoken, have foretold these days" (Acts 3:24). Later Peter would write that the suffering, sin-bearing mission of the servant had been fulfilled in Jesus' death; "by his wounds you have been healed" (1 Peter 2:21–24; Isa. 53:5, 12).

On the Gaza road Philip chatted with an Ethiopian official, a proselyte who had been to Jerusalem to worship. The man was reading from the servant passages in Isaiah. "Who is the prophet talking about?" he asked Philip. Philip took that very passage about the suffering servant and explained to the Ethiopian the good news about Jesus (Acts 8:26–35).

Paul proclaimed the same message: "What God promised our fathers he has fulfilled for us, their children" (Acts 13:32–33). Included in this fulfilment were "the holy and sure blessings promised to David" (Acts 13:34; Isa. 55:3). The universal mission of the servant of the Lord had been inaugurated, a mission to which the apostles now were joined (Acts 13:47; Isa. 49:5–6). It is also likely that Paul's great hymn of Jesus' humiliation and exaltation (Phil. 2:6–11) intentionally reflects the mission of the servant who would be humiliated and killed (Isa. 52:14; 53:3–9), but in the end would see the light of life (Isa. 53:11). At last, every knee would bow before the Lord (Isa. 45:22–25)!

The Fulfilment Motif in the Apostles

As they explained the inauguration of the time of fulfilment, the apostles drew deeply from the well of the Hebrew prophets. The promise of restoration to David's dynasty had come to pass in the kingship of Jesus (Acts 15:16; Amos 9:11). The promise that the Israelites would possess the remnant of Edom was fulfilled as the gospel of Jesus was preached to the Gentiles (Acts 15:17; Amos 9:12). Anna anticipated the redemption of Jerusalem in the birth of Jesus (Luke 2:38; see also Isa. 52:1–12). Paul went on to interpret this redemption in spiritual terms. The good news upon the mountains that was proclaimed to Zion had become the preaching of the gospel of Jesus Christ (Isa. 52:7; Rom. 10:14–15). The Jerusalem which was free was the Jerusalem from above (Isa. 52:9–10; Gal. 4:26). The exiles' departure from pagan Babylon to return to ancient Jerusalem symbolized the Christians' departure from the world of sin to the New Jerusalem (Isa. 52:11; 2 Cor. 6:17; Rev. 18:4; 21:2, 10).

Isaiah's poetic conflation of the holy mountain, the holy city, and the holy people reaches its climax in the Apocalypse of John, where the people of God are described as a triumphant throng on heavenly Mount Zion (Rev. 14:1–5), and later as the bride of the Lamb, the holy city, New Jerusalem (Rev. 21). John had no doubts that he was already living in the closing hours. Though he pictured the climax of the age in vivid apocalyptic imagery filled with ambiguous symbolism, he was very clear that what he wrote about "must soon take place" (Rev. 1:1), for "the time is near" (Rev. 1:3; 22:10). The last words of the New Testament look to the second coming of Jesus as "soon" (Rev. 22:7, 12, 20).

The Remnant

What about the predictions concerning the remnant of Israel who would be cleansed and restored, and the remnant of the nations who would come to worship Yahweh, the king of the whole earth? Here, too, the days of fulfilment had begun! From Solomon's Porch Peter boldly announced that the first beneficiaries of the promise that all the families of the earth would be blessed in Abraham and his seed had been the Jews of Jerusalem: "You are heirs of the prophets and of the covenant God made with your fathers" (Acts 3:25). God "sent [Jesus] first to you

to bless you by turning each of you from your wicked ways" (Acts 3:26).
Paul, however, would make explicit that the seed of Abraham must be
defined in terms of faith, not ethnicity. The seed of Abraham to whom
the promise referred was first of all Jesus Christ (Gal. 3:16). Thereafter
it included all those who come to faith in Jesus: "If you belong to Christ,
then you are Abraham's seed, and heirs according to the promise" (Gal.
3:29). The ancient promise to Abraham was nothing less than the gospel
to the nations announced in advance to Abraham so that they might be
"blessed along with Abraham, the man of faith" (Gal. 3:9). So, as Paul
reasons to the Romans, "Not all who are descended from Israel are Israel.
Nor because they are his descendants are they all Abraham's children"
(Rom. 9:6–7; see also 2:28–29). Rather, the true children of Abraham,
who are heirs of the promise, are not his natural descendants, but his
spiritual ones (Rom. 9:8; Gal. 3:7); and in that sense Abraham is the
father of all who embrace the faith of Jesus Christ (Rom. 4:9–12, 16–17,
22–24; cf. Gal. 4:28–31). Paul ends the Galatian letter by referring to
the New Testament Christians as the "Israel of God" (Gal. 6:16). With
this conclusion the writer of Hebrews agrees (Heb. 6:13–18).

It may well be asked what criteria determine if an Old Testament
prophecy was to be fulfilled in Jesus' day or at the end of the age. The
most important criterion surely must be the interpretations of the apostles themselves. Inasmuch as the apostles were writing under the guid-
ance of the Spirit, their interpretations of prophetic fulfilment are
vouched for by God. Of course, there are a considerable number of
prophecies about which the apostles gave no opinion; however, the many
cases where they did give an opinion clearly demonstrate that in their
view the last days had begun with the birth, ministry, death, and resurrection of Jesus.

Transfer of Jewish Vocabulary to Christians

IN PAUL

Given the conclusion that, with regard to prophetic fulfilment, true
Jewishness was primarily a spiritual, not merely a genealogical matter, it
is not surprising that the apostles and writers of the New Testament frequently use Jewish vocabulary to describe Christians. Paul, for instance,
can take the prophecy of Hosea about the restoration of the northern
nation and apply it directly to the conversion of Gentiles to Christianity. The rejection and promised reclamation of the northern Israelites
find fulfilment in the Gentiles who once were not God's people, but now
have become his people (Rom. 9:24–26; Eph. 2:11–3:6; Hos. 1:10;

2:23). Furthermore, Isaiah's description of the remnant of Judah to be saved has its fulfilment in the Gentiles who, although they did not pursue righteousness, have obtained a righteousness by faith (Rom. 9:27–30). Joel's prediction about the last days has now come to pass: "Everyone who calls on the name of the Lord will be saved" (Rom. 10:12–13; Joel 2:32). The Gentiles have been grafted into the tree of Israel (Rom. 11:17, 24); thus all who belong to the Israel of faith, whether natural descendants or spiritual ones, will be saved (Rom. 11:26–27; Gal. 6:16; cf. Isa. 59:20–21).

In Peter

Peter similarly draws from the rich vocabulary of Jewishness in his letter to the Christians in Pontus, Galatia, Cappadocia, Asia, and Bithynia. He begins by addressing them with three very Jewish titles, "the chosen," "the resident aliens," and "the diaspora" (1 Peter 1:1–2; 2:11). While this vocabulary has sociological significance in denoting Christians who, though widely scattered throughout the world, maintained a solidarity of faith and suffering as they awaited the return of the Lord, it also has theological significance. Peter seems to imply, sometimes subtly and sometimes overtly, that true Jews are those who have faith in Jesus Christ. They are the ones with a "living hope" for "an inheritance that can never perish" (1 Peter 1:3–4). The land grant of Canaan to Israel now has its counterpart in the Christian inheritance, which, unlike the former, "can never perish, spoil or fade" since it is "kept in heaven" (1 Peter 1:4).

Peter then proceeds to point out that the Hebrew prophets' predictions regarding the days of eschatological salvation were actually given in service to the Christian church (1 Peter 1:10–12). Thus the commandments in Leviticus about holiness (Lev. 11:44–45; 19:2; 20:7) now become imperatives for Christians (1 Peter 1:16). And like the ancient Israelites, Christians now live as resident aliens in a pagan world (1 Peter 1:17; 2:11; cf. Deut. 23:7). Moreover, the Jewish Passover has been fulfilled in the Christian Passover of the death of Jesus, God's unblemished Lamb (1 Peter 1:18–19; see also 1 Cor. 5:7). This Lamb, chosen before the creation, has been revealed "in these last times" (1 Peter 1:20).

In vocabulary deliberately borrowed from Old Testament Israel, Peter goes on to describe Christians as the new people of God. The body of Christians is the new temple, not built out of quarried limestone, but constructed from "living stones" (1 Peter 2:5a). They form a new "holy priesthood, offering spiritual sacrifices" (1 Peter 2:5b). In a collage of citations from the Old Testament, Peter applies directly to the Christian church language which originally was applied to Old Testament Israel. It is not that Peter denies the initial intent of these passages. He certainly was aware that they were originally directed toward ancient Israel and her own historical circumstances. However, in light of the Jesus event these passages have taken on new and greater meaning. The tested cornerstone of Zion, once a metaphor for the faithfulness of Yahweh in the vicissitudes of politics in the eighth century B.C., has now become a metaphor for Jesus Christ (1 Peter 2:6; Isa. 28:16). The stumbling stone, once a metaphor for Yahweh's strange actions in the realpolitik of the ancient Near East (Isa. 8:14), now refers to Christ, the rock of offense over which unbelievers stumble (1 Peter 2:7–8). Peter sees these Old Testament stone metaphors as types of the New Testament stone, Jesus! Unlike skeptics and unbelievers who stumble over the New Testament stone, Peter's readers have come to genuine faith. Even though they are not of Jewish descent, they have become the new people of God. Just as the ancient people of Israel were once called a chosen people (Isa. 43:20), a royal house (2 Sam. 7:11b–13), a body of priests, a holy nation (Exod. 19:6), and God's treasured possession (Exod. 19:5; Deut. 4:20; 7:6; 14:2), so now the body of Christians carries those distinctions (1 Peter 2:9). They have been reclaimed out of the exile of estrangement from God. The ancient promises to Israel have been fulfilled in the salvation of Gentiles (1 Peter 2:10; Hos. 1:10; 2:23).

Given Peter's transfer of vocabulary from ancient Israel to the Christian church, it is hard for us to escape the conclusion that he intends his Christian readers to understand themselves as God's remnant. The kingdoms of Israel and Judah having proved not to be the kingdom of God, the church has now become God's royal house. Jesus, the royal Son, has ascended to the throne! Yahweh had promised to build for David a house and a kingdom; the Christian community is heir to that promise. The church has also received Israel's commission of priesthood to the nations through the gospel. For it had been promised that after Israel's collective failure to become a nation of priests reached its climax in the broken covenant and exile, a remnant of exiles would be assigned this priestly ministry (Isa. 61:6). The church is that remnant!

IN THE BOOK OF HEBREWS

The Book of Hebrews, like 1 Peter, employs the language of Israel to describe the spiritual realities of Christian faith. God's final word, spoken in the last days, has been given through his Son (Heb. 1:1–2). Jesus is the high priest whom Christians confess (Heb. 3:1), greater than Moses (3:3) and greater than Aaron's sons (Heb. 7:1–11; 8:6). The promise of rest was not attained by Joshua's conquest of Canaan, but by the preaching of the gospel (Heb. 3:16–4:8). The weekly Sabbath finds its counterpart in the rest which Jesus gives (Heb. 4:8–11). The old sacrificial system has come to an end because the better sacrifice of God's Son has accomplished forever what the old could never do (Heb. 9:11–10:18). The Most Holy Place is no longer on Mount Zion in Jerusalem; rather, it is the immediate spiritual access Christians have to God because of the priestly work of Christ (Heb. 10:19–22). Christians come to Mount Zion, to be sure, but it is not the hill near Jerusalem (Heb. 12:22–24). Abraham may have been promised Canaan, but to his eyes of faith even the Promised Land was like a "foreign country." For Canaan was certainly not what God's promise was ultimately about (Heb. 11:9–10, 13–16). Therefore the writer encourages Christians to go to Jesus "outside the camp," that is to say, outside the traditional structures of Judaism (Heb. 13:12–14).

IN THE BOOK OF REVELATION

The final book of the New Testament carries this transfer of vocabulary to its climax. There is a remarkable reversal of symbolism so that what once was considered exclusively Jewish has now been fully appropriated by the Christian church. True Jewishness no longer resides in an ethnic pedigree (Rev. 2:9; 3:9). The menorah, which once belonged to the old temple, now represents the Christian churches (Rev. 1:12, 20). The great altar is no longer a place of animal sacrifices, but the residence of the souls of the Christian martyrs (Rev. 6:9). Their prayers have replaced the incense of the Jewish temple now lying in ruins (Rev. 5:8; 6:10–11; 8:3–4). The pillars in the temple are victorious Christians (Rev. 3:12). The real temple, with its ark of the covenant, is in heaven (Rev. 11:19). The priests are those washed in the blood of the Lamb who serve God in his heavenly temple (Rev. 1:6; 5:9–10; 7:14–15). And because of its rejection of Jesus the Messiah, ancient Jerusalem, where God had once set his sacred name, has now become Sodom and Egypt, the very epitome of blasphemy (Rev. 11:8). In its place is the vision of a New Jerusalem coming down from heaven (Rev. 3:12; 21:2, 10).

The Present-Day Framework of the Question

We began this chapter with the question "Are we living in the last days?" From the foregoing survey of how the vocabulary and concepts relating to the last days developed, and especially how the New Testament Christians interpreted the predictions of the Old Testament prophets, we are in a much better position to give an answer.

Three Questionable Assumptions

When contemporary Christians ask whether we are living in the last days, they often make one or more of three questionable assumptions. The first is that the earliest Christians, having anticipated a lengthy church age, which has now been nearly two millennia, framed their teachings about the future and the end of the age accordingly. It is assumed that Jesus' words in passages such as the Olivet Discourse (Matt. 24–25; Mark 13; Luke 21) were left to the apostles as a depository of information about the closing hours of the age, information that would not become relevant for a very long time. The same assumption is made about the eschatological passages in the letters of Paul, Peter, and John. It is even more pronounced in interpretations of the Apocalypse of John, where it is quite common for readers to assume that, barring chapters 2 and 3, the book has virtually nothing to say to the church at the end of the first century. Instead, it is a repository of details about a distant future. When the question "Are we living in the last days?" is laden with this assumption, it usually means, "Given that the writers of the New Testament knew that the church age would be very long, what clues exist in their writings to help us decipher whether or not we are now living near the close of the Christian Era?"

The second questionable assumption is that the Bible provides specific indicators which signal the last hours of the age. These indicators, usually called "signs of the times," are believed to be natural disasters, political turmoil, and general moral decline. The tendency is to say, "Look, since 'such and such' is happening, doesn't that mean we are living in the last days?" The escalation of wars, earthquakes, diseases, famines, technological advances, the statehood of Israel, the development of the European Economic Community (now the European Union), and the appearance of various political despots all are believed to be direct evidence that the close of the age is upon us. In fact, however, Jesus said that natural disasters and international turmoil would be "birth pains," not signs (Mark 13:8).

The third questionable assumption is a matter of misplaced perspective. Those who hold it stand in the sandals of the Old Testament person as though the days of fulfilment were primarily ahead of them. They do not appreciate the full implications of the fact that the Jesus event is a fulfilment of prophecy. They miss the broad interpretive principle that the Jesus event and the establishment of the new people of faith marked the dawn of the fulfilment of all that the prophets had said (Luke 24:25–27). The last days have already begun. The future age is not merely somewhere in the future, but, in fact, the future age is already imping-ing upon the present age!

When these three assumptions frame the question "Are we living in the last days?" they misdirect the questioner. Consider, for example, the assumption that the earliest Christians expected the Christian Era to be lengthy. This assumption is at least doubtful if not altogether inaccurate. Perhaps the clearest example is the rumor among some disciples that John, the beloved disciple, would not die but would live to see the return of the Lord (John 21:21–23). If it was commonly believed, even though mistakenly, that the second coming of Jesus might take place within the lifetime of someone living in the first century, one can hardly conclude that the earliest Christians anticipated a lengthy church age. The repeated statements in the New Testament about the nearness of the return of the Lord also suggest that the earliest Christians did not look for a lengthy church age. The hour had come for them to "wake up," because "sal-vation is nearer now than when we first believed" (Rom. 13:11; see also 1 Thess. 5:1–11). The "night is nearly over; the day is almost here," Paul said (Rom. 13:12a). Accordingly, his converts "eagerly wait[ed] for our Lord Jesus Christ to be revealed" (1 Cor. 1:7–8; see also Phil. 3:20–21). In fact, Paul could even suggest that married people might just as well live as if they were single, since the present age was already "passing away" (1 Cor. 7:29–31).

The words of the apostles indicate they believed themselves to be in the final hours of the age. "The Lord is near," they said (Phil. 4:5), and the Judge is "at the door" (James 5:7–9). "Dear children, this is the last hour . . . even now many antichrists have come. This is how we know it is the last hour," John wrote (1 John 2:18). Paul anticipated that he might be among those who would be alive at the return of Christ (1 Thess. 4:15–18; Titus 2:13). The Thessalonians took him so seriously that they even wondered if local persecutions might mean that the day of the Lord had already arrived (2 Thess. 2:1–12). Though Paul corrected their mis-apprehension, elsewhere he stated his belief that God would "soon crush Satan," a reference to the earliest messianic promise in the Bible (Rom. 16:20; Gen. 3:15). To be sure, Paul also anticipated that some Chris-tians would die before the return of Christ (1 Thess. 4:13–18), and he also considered the possibility that he himself might die (Phil. 1:20–24). Still, the final hope was that "whether we are awake or asleep, we may live together with him" (1 Thess. 5:10). Jesus' own teaching implied that his return was always to be considered impending, since the hour was unknown (Matt. 24:36–25:13). In the Apocalypse of John are repeated warnings that the Lord was coming *tachy,* that is, speedily or without delay (Rev. 2:16; 3:11; 22:7, 12, 20). "Maranatha," an Aramaic expression from the early church meaning "Our Lord, come," cogently expressed this longing and hope (1 Cor. 16:22).

The Overlapping of Present and Future

The questionable assumption that the apostles and disciples anticipated a lengthy church age leads to another misconception, namely, that because the promises about the end of the age belonged to the far-flung future, they were irrelevant to the earliest Christians. In fact, however, the earliest Christians considered the time of fulfilment to have dawned already with the coming of Jesus. They saw themselves as the generation "on whom the fulfillment of the ages has come" (1 Cor. 10:11). In their view the Messiah had appeared "once for all at the end of the ages" (Heb. 9:26). This is not to say, of course, that the apostles considered that everything was now completed. As we shall see, they patently did not think so. However, their perspective of the transition in the ages was unique, as a number of contemporary biblical scholars have pointed out. They believed that the future age had begun in the Jesus event before the present age had run out. Thus their viewpoint was that the ages overlapped. The future and the present were so intertwined that the believer in Jesus Christ stood, as it were, with one foot in the present age and the other in the future age.

One first sees this overlapping of the present and the future in the teachings of Jesus about the kingdom of God. The Evangelists' vocabulary is striking in that it describes the kingdom as both something near and yet something at the end. Both John the Baptizer and Jesus proclaimed the kingdom of heaven a present reality.[11] It was "near" (Matt. 3:2; 4:17), and so Jesus preached the "good news of the kingdom" in

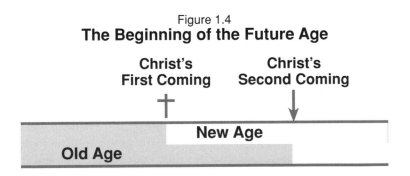

Figure 1.4
The Beginning of the Future Age

the various villages of Galilee (Matt. 4:23; Luke 4:43). His counsel to Nicodemus that he must be "born again" to "enter the kingdom of God" seems to refer to something possible at that very moment (John 3:3–7). Further, Jesus sent out his disciples to proclaim the same message (Matt. 10:7; Luke 10:9, 11). This task of proclamation would continue as a testimony to the nations until the very end (Matt. 24:14). In explaining the kingdom of God to his disciples (Mark 4:11), Jesus said that the message of the kingdom was like seed planted in human hearts (Mark 4:3; Matt. 13:19, 24, 38). It was like treasure in a field which men and women could find, or like a costly pearl which they could buy (Matt. 13:44–46). To a scribe who perceived the meaning of his teaching, Jesus said, "You are not far from the kingdom of God" (Mark 12:34), and to the Pharisees who asked when the kingdom of God would come, Jesus said, "The kingdom is within [among] you" (Luke 17:20–21).[12] In addition, the fact that Jesus exercised authority over the power of Satan was, in his own words, a sign that "the kingdom of God has come upon you" (Matt. 12:28; Luke 11:20; see also Luke 9:1–2). More to the point, Jesus clearly taught that in his death and resurrection he would face the eschatological battle with the evil one, and Satan would be driven out while the world would be judged (John 12:31; 14:30; 16:11).

At the same time, the kingdom of God was both present and future. The eschatological feast of the kingdom was still to come (Matt. 8:11; Luke 12:35–48; 22:29–30). To those who thought that it would appear immediately, Jesus gave a parable showing it would not be consummated until his return (Luke 19:11–27). In fact, the disciples would experience a time of longing for the Messiah before he returned (Luke 17:22–24). He would come back, however (Luke 21:27–31)! A great judgment would distinguish between those to whom the kingdom was given and those who were to be shut out (Luke 13:28–29; Matt. 7:21–23; 13:37–43, 47–50; 25:31–34, 41). Consequently, in his Sermon on the Mount Jesus called his followers to a higher interpretation of the law, since the reward for their discipleship would be the eschatological kingdom of heaven (Matt. 5:3, 10–12, 20; 6:19–21, 33). He also taught the disciples to pray for the coming of the kingdom (Luke 11:2; Matt. 6:10).[13]

The overlapping of the present and the future is a distinctive feature of Pauline theology as well. In the Pauline letters, salvation is described in three tenses. It is at once a past event, a present experience, and a future hope:[14] we "were saved" (Rom. 8:24), we "are being saved" (1 Cor. 15:2), and we "shall be saved" (Rom. 5:9). In fact, Paul can use all three tenses in the same thought: "we have been justified . . . we have peace . . . we rejoice in the hope of the glory of God" (Rom. 5:1–2). On the one hand, Paul can say that already we have been rescued from the present evil age and the dominion of darkness, and already we have been transferred over into the kingdom of God's Son (Gal. 1:4; Col. 1:13). Already the evil powers of the age have been disarmed and conquered by the cross (Col. 2:15). Death has been destroyed, and life and immortality have been given (2 Tim. 1:10). Already believers are "in the heavenly realms" where Christ has been seated at the Father's right hand (Eph. 1:3, 20; 2:6). Already they are "a new creation," having experienced the power of resurrection life (2 Cor. 5:17; Rom. 6:4; Col. 3:1). The day of salvation toward which the prophets looked is "now" (2 Cor. 6:2). Eschatological acquittal already has been pronounced for those who believe (Rom. 3:21–26; 5:1).

At the same time, Paul urges his converts to look to the future. The day of the Lord is coming (1 Thess. 5:2; 2 Thess. 1:10; 2:2; 1 Cor. 1:8; 5:5; 2 Cor. 1:14; Phil. 1:6, 10; 2:16; 2 Tim. 1:18)! Paul uses three words to describe the advent of Christ at the end of the age. It is his *parousia,* that is, his arrival or presence (1 Cor. 15:23; 1 Thess. 2:19; 3:13; 4:15; 5:23; 2 Thess. 2:1, 8). It is his *apokalypsis,* his unveiling or disclosure (1 Cor. 1:7; 2 Thess. 1:7). It is his *epiphaneia,* his appearing (2 Thess. 2:8; 1 Tim. 6:14; 2 Tim. 4:1, 8; Titus 2:13). Christians are called to "wait for [God's] Son from heaven" (1 Thess. 1:10; 2:19; 3:13). Some intermediate events remain, such as the great rebellion and the rise of the eschatological man of lawlessness (2 Thess. 2:1–12). At last, however, the dead in Christ will be resurrected to welcome the Lord in his return to the earth (1 Cor. 15:50–55; 1 Thess. 4:13–17). There will be a great judgment; some will be "counted worthy of the kingdom of God" while others will be "shut out from the presence of the Lord" (2 Thess. 1:5–10; Rom. 2:5–8, 16). Then "the end will come," when Christ will hand the kingdom over to the Father after all opposition has been destroyed (1 Cor. 15:22–28; Col. 1:20; Phil. 2:10–11). Yes, as Paul says, there is a "present age," and there is an "age to come" (Eph. 1:21). Yet, as another New Testament writer puts it, Christians in the present age have already "tasted . . . the powers of the coming age" (Heb. 6:5).

This paradoxical overlapping of the present and the future, sometimes called "the already, not yet" tension, demonstrates that the earliest Christians in fact did not view eschatological categories to be irrelevant to themselves. For them, the last days had already dawned in the coming of Jesus. Jesus was the Messiah anticipated by the prophets. The wonderful benefits of the new age, such as salvation and acquittal, the gift of the Spirit, the enthronement of God's people, the dethronement

of the worldly powers of evil, the gift of eternal life, and the inauguration of the kingdom of God, were already the present experience of
Christians. With the ascension of the Lord to the Father's right hand,
the messianic reign had begun (Rom. 5:17, 21; 1 Cor. 15:25; Eph.
1:20–21; Phil. 2:9)! Still, the old age had not yet reached its consummation, nor would it until the return of the Lord. Between the enthronement of Christ at the Father's right hand and the Lord's second coming, believers experience eschatology, and at the same time they anticipate
eschatology. They live in both the present and the future. Already they
are in the last days, yet the day of the Lord is still to come.

This interim eschatology, in which both the fulfilled and the unful-
filled exist side by side, means that the Christian interpreter cannot stand
in the sandals of the Old Testament person as though the messianic age
lies totally in the future. The messianic age has already begun, and it is
already present in a powerful way. However, while the kingdom of God
certainly has been inaugurated in the first advent of Christ, it has not
been consummated. The entire period between the enthronement of
the ascended Christ in the heavens, where he must remain until the time
for God to restore everything, and his second coming, when he will save
his people and judge the world, must be recognized as the last days (Acts
3:20–21).

The Beginning of the Last Days: The First Coming of Jesus

The fulfilment of all that the prophets spoke has already dawned (Luke
24:25–27). The "fulfillment of the ages" has begun (1 Cor. 10:11)! "In
these last days" God has spoken by his Son (Heb. 1:2)! The Messiah
already has "appeared . . . at the end of the ages" (Heb. 9:26). His power
over Satan is evidence that "the kingdom of God has come upon you"
(Matt. 12:28). Messiah's reign has begun, and "he must reign until he
has put all his enemies under his feet" (1 Cor. 15:25; Rom. 16:20; Phil.
2:9–11). The messianic Spirit that was promised for the last days has
also been given, for, as Peter said, "This is what was spoken" (Acts
2:16–17). Already believers have been rescued "from the present evil
age" (Gal. 1:4), and already they have been transferred over into "the
kingdom of the Son" (Col. 1:13). The present age is already "passing
away" (1 Cor. 7:31)! "The night is nearly over; the day is almost here"
(Rom. 13:12a). "The darkness is passing and the true light is already
shining" (1 John 2:8). "This is the last hour" (1 John 2:18). "The Lord
is near" (Phil. 4:5), and "the Judge is standing at the door!" (James
5:7–9). The New Testament closes near the end of the first century A.D.

with the repeated warning that the Lord's coming is soon (Rev. 2:16; 3:11; 22:7, 12, 20).

Are we living in the last days? In light of the teaching of the apostles, the question must be answered with an unequivocal yes, for the last days have been upon us since the advent of Jesus the Messiah almost two millennia ago!

Should Christians Try
to Predict Christ's Return?

e concluded in the first chapter that the time of messianic fulfilment has already dawned, and that therefore the people of faith have been in the last days since the time of Jesus. We will now explore whether the length of the period between the first and second comings of Christ can be calculated. Given that the apostolic church did not attempt to date the return of the Lord, and given that they necessarily had to revise their expectation that he might return in their own lifetimes, we might ask whether there are any clues that might suggest how long before he returns. Many Christians answer yes to this question. They believe that built into the Bible's testimony about history and the future are indications which, if carefully exposed and interpreted, will yield an approximation, if not a precise date, for the second coming of Jesus. How valid this belief may be is the burden of this chapter.

Some Historical Perspective

The attempt to predict the time of God's final intervention in history is not a recent phenomenon. In fact, one almost could say that it is a time-honored tradition, since so many Christians and, before them, Jews have made the effort.

Jewish Apocalyptic

In the intertestamental period (about 450 B.C. to the birth of Jesus) a new literary genre developed. The roots of Jewish apocalyptic are found in some portions of the writing prophets, such as Isaiah, Ezekiel, Zechariah, and Daniel. However, the full-blown style of apocalyptic, which aimed at elucidating present crises in light of the imminent end of the age, reached its zenith in the two centuries prior to the time of Jesus. While we do not know the extent to which the various Jewish groups made use of apocalyptic literature, the Qumran community, which produced the Dead Sea Scrolls, certainly valued it highly. As a literary style apocalyptic exhibited features of special revelation, unveiling the secrets of the invisible realm through dreams, visions, and heavenly journeys with angelic guides. Apocalyptic usually took the form of theodicy, that is, an explanation of why the world seemed to be locked in deadly combat between the forces of good and evil.

Jewish apocalyptic featured a marked dualism of the ages, with the present age, as it drew to a close, hopelessly given over to the powers of evil. The future age was about to commence through divine intervention. Soon God would put down evil once and for all, so that he might inaugurate a new age of blessedness. It was frequently declared that the old earth would be replaced by a new one. As the old age was in its death throes, there would be marked activity by angels and demons. Good angels, the guardians of the nations, would war with the demons, the fallen angels on the side of Satan. In apocalyptic, cosmic disturbances are prominent, including the shaking of the earth's foundations, the opening of the doors of the underworld, the roaring of the oceans, and a host of natural disasters. Even the heavenly bodies are disturbed, and there are universal calamity and woe.

Some of the apocalypses describe a messiah-like figure called the Son of man. The Son of man stands in opposition to a champion of evil, an antichrist sometimes depicted as a human and other times as a mythological monster or the incarnation of a demon. In the end God will triumph! While there was unmitigated pessimism regarding the present age, there was great hope for the future, since God was on the verge of intervening in human history.

Jewish apocalyptic arose against the background of the community's troubles with the Greek and Roman political machines, pagan culture, and corruption in the temple, a background that is somewhat different from Christian apocalyptic. Nevertheless, New Testament allusions to apocalyptic sources are indications of common strands between Jewish and Christian apocalyptic. The clearest examples are in Jude and 2 Peter.

When these epistles speak of the angels who sinned and are now bound in chains (Jude 6; 2 Peter 2:4), they are referring to extensive apocalyptic commentaries on Genesis 6:1–4 (1 Enoch 86–88; 106.13–14; Jubilees 4.15; 5.1–11; Testament of Reuben 5.6; Testament of Naphtali 3.5; 2 Enoch 7, 18; 2 Baruch 56.10–16). Similarly, Peter's description of the righteousness of Lot (2 Peter 2:7–8) comes not from Genesis, but the apocryphal Book of Wisdom (10.6). Michael's confrontation with Satan (Jude 9) comes from the lost ending of a writing called the Assumption of Moses. The reference to an eschatological judgment of the world by fire (2 Peter 3:10) also shows a knowledge of apocalyptic (Life of Adam and Eve 49.3; Sibylline Oracles 3.54, 543, 690; 2 Baruch 27.10; 70.8). Finally, Jude's description of Enoch's vision (Jude 14–15) is a partial quotation from 1 Enoch 1.9, while the designation of Enoch as the "seventh from Adam" is also an apocalyptic tradition (1 Enoch 60.8; 93.3; Jubilees 7.39).[1]

The attempt to predict the time of the end rests upon the apocalyptic belief that world history is divided into great epochs. The succession of these epochs forms the scheme of history. The Book of Jubilees, for instance, reckons the epochs on the basis of the Old Testament jubilee, and it calculates the end by summing up how many jubilees are expected in the whole of world history. The Assumption of Moses does much the same sort of calculation. First Enoch, on the other hand, figures the scheme of history from Noah's flood to the great judgment to be seventy generations. The Testament of Abraham reckons the history of the world to be seven millennia corresponding to the seven days of creation. All of these literary efforts aimed at discovering how much longer the world would carry on before history reached its climax. Regardless of the technique employed, the intent of the apocalyptists was to predict how close they were to the end. The community at Qumran expected the end to culminate with a war between the sons of light and the sons of darkness. In this war the righteous members of Qumran would join forces with God and the angels to fight their enemies, who were allied with Belial. Since even then they were experiencing severe distress, they believed that the eschatological war was near.

Christian Speculation

Postapostolic Christians were not slow in imitating Jewish apocalyptic, though with the difference that it was now Jesus Christ who would intervene in human history. In the Epistle of Barnabas (ca. A.D. 100), the six days of creation correspond to six thousand years of human history, after which is expected a millennium of rest (Barnabas 15). Since the age of the world at that time was thought to be nearing six thousand years, the end was expected within a couple of centuries.[2] This six-day schematic was also advocated by other Christians in the early centuries of the church.[3] Of course, some predictions about the return of Christ were wildly speculative, like the ecstatic prophecies of Montanus that the New Jerusalem was about to descend upon Pepuza, Phrygia. Nevertheless, apocalyptic speculation did not disappear.

In the Middle Ages, various attempts were made to predict the end, especially as history neared the close of the first millennium A.D. Some projected that the world would end when the Feast of the Annunciation coincided with Good Friday in A.D. 992. New Year's Eve, A.D. 999, was believed by many to be doomsday. Some Christians, on the basis of Revelation 20:7–8, believed that Satan was to be loosed upon the world exactly a thousand years after the birth of Jesus. All sorts of omens and portents, from eclipses to meteors to volcanic eruptions and other natural disasters, were heralded as signs of the end. When the year A.D. 1000 passed without graves opening, life resumed its normal pace, at least until A.D. 1033, which was reckoned to be the thousandth year after Jesus' crucifixion. Joachim of Fiore, a twelfth-century Italian monk, calculated that the last age of history would begin about A.D. 1260, a calculation apparently based on the biblical references to the number 1,260 or its equivalents (Dan. 7:25; 9:27; 12:7; Rev. 11:2–3, 9; 12:6, 14; 13:5). The Crusades were in part fueled by the belief that the world would end soon. Since it was believed that Christ would not return until the world was converted to the faith of Christianity, the wars were intended to hasten Christ's return. Unbelievers were to be converted or destroyed. Later still, Anabaptist Protestants in the 1500s concluded that Martin Luther was the Antichrist and that the millennial kingdom was about to begin. The peasants of Germany would rule the world from Münster, the site of the New Jerusalem.

And so it has continued. Predictions and schematics about the end have certainly not been wanting! To borrow a line from the Book of Hebrews, "The time would fail me to tell of" the Taborites, the Hussites, the Fifth Monarchists, Christopher Columbus, the First Great Awakening, the Shakers, the Latter-day Saints, William Miller, Ellen G. White, the Jehovah's Witnesses, and John Nelson Darby. The list could be considerably expanded from just the last couple of decades of the twentieth century! If nothing else, the plethora of failed calculations should make the contemporary Christian wary of accepting too quickly the latest schematic to come down the apocalyptic pipeline. With such caution in mind, we now turn more directly to the question "Should Christians attempt to predict the time of Christ's return?"

Can the Length of the Church Age Be Calculated?

It is accepted by virtually all schools within conservative Christian theology that the church age will end with the second coming of Jesus Christ. Thus, if one could calculate how long the church age will last, one also could know approximately when Christ will return. As we have already seen, numerous attempts to calculate the length of the church age have been made through the centuries. While some of them must be described as eccentric or even bizarre, a few merit more serious consideration.

The Theory of Epochs

A recurring and popular schematic is to view the history of the world in terms of epochs matching the days of creation. It is pointed out that Scripture says, "With the Lord a day is like a thousand years, and a thousand years are like a day" (2 Peter 3:8). If God's work of creation occupied six days, with the seventh day set aside for rest, then the history of humans might last six thousand years, with the seventh day set aside for the millennium as a type of Sabbath. Those who follow the traditional chronology of James Ussher (1581–1656), the Irish scholar and archbishop of Armagh whose dating system was inserted in the marginal notes of the King James Version, may regard the year A.D. 2000 as the end of the six days of human history. Ussher calculated from the genealogical tables in Genesis and elsewhere that creation took place in 4004 B.C. Now if creation can be fixed at about 4004 B.C., then the six days of human history will be complete in approximately A.D. 2000. The Lord will return, ushering in the millennial day of rest.

One of the most popular teachings of this sort was developed early in the twentieth century by Clarence Larkin of Philadelphia, though it is likely he relied on the similar efforts of others before him. His primary work has been reprinted many times and was still in print more than seventy-five years after its initial copyright in 1918. Though allowing for a certain amount of confusion in the calendars, Larkin still concluded, "If our inference is correct, then it follows that the Return of the Lord will take place before the close of this present century."[4]

How sound is this schematic? While on the surface it may seem plausible enough, there are significant reasons why Christians should be wary. First, hardly any living evangelical scholars, not to mention nonevangelical scholars, are willing to accept the chronology of Archbishop Ussher, in spite of the fact that a few Bibles still print his dates in the margins. On the basis of the idiomatic usage of the Hebrew verb *yālad* ("to become the father of") it is widely accepted among all scholars that there are significant gaps in the genealogies (i.e., they do not always proceed from father to son, but sometimes move from ancestor to descendant). There are, to be sure, evangelical scholars who argue for a young earth (i.e., less than ten thousand years old), but once one moves away from the 4004 B.C. date for creation, even if only a thousand years, the whole schematic falls flat. If creation occurred in, say, 5000 B.C., Christ should have returned long ago! Beyond that, many evangelicals question the young-earth theory on theological, exegetical, and scientific grounds.

Second, when one looks carefully at the passage in 2 Peter, it is highly doubtful whether Peter is attempting to provide a key for computing the length of historical epochs. The passage is Peter's response to scoffers who failed to consider that time is not the same for God as it is for us. These heretics, for so we may call them, had given up altogether on the promise that Christ would return, since his coming seemed to be later than they had supposed (2 Peter 3:3–4). In response, Peter reflects upon the psalmist's words, "For a thousand years in your sight are like a day that has just gone by, or like a watch in the night" (Ps. 90:4). In doing so, he points out that human standards are inappropriate for calculating divine appointments. If the return of Christ seemed to be delayed, it was not due to divine tardiness, but human miscalculation (2 Peter 3:9a). The perceived delay in Christ's coming, far from being a delinquency on God's part, was a demonstration of his patience and mercy (2 Peter 3:9b, 15a).

If Peter had wanted to provide a cryptic key for solving the riddle of time along the lines of a parallel between the creative days and the epochs of human history, why did he not appeal to apocalyptic literature, which already offered that very type of calculation? Instead, Peter appealed to the psalms, where a thousand years is compared with a day or even one of the night watches. At most, this statement is a simile pointing to God's sovereignty over time. Further, as Derek Kidner has pointed out, it is similar to Isaiah 40:15, "where the nations are 'like a drop from a bucket, and . . . as the dust on the scales.'"[5] In the end, this schematic to calculate the length of the church era must be rejected as unsound.

The Theory of Church Ages

An entirely different sort of schematic, which also suggests an approximate length of the church era, arose in the dispensational treatment of the seven churches in Asia Minor mentioned in the Apocalypse of John

(Rev. 2–3). Using the commonly accepted idea that the number seven signifies completion, some interpreters argued that the seven congregations represent seven periods of church history from apostolic times up to the end. John, then, was allowed a preview of church history: Ephesus, the apostolic church; Smyrna, the persecuted church; Pergamum, the worldly church; Thyatira, the church of the Dark Ages; Sardis, the church of the Reformation; Philadelphia, the missionary church; and Laodicea, the apostate church. The suggestion was offered that the final epoch of church history is twentieth-century apostate Christendom. While most of those advocating this theory did not attempt to date the end of the church era precisely, they argued that Christendom might well be in the closing epoch of Laodicea, and therefore the return of Christ is upon us.

Perhaps the most remarkable thing about this theory is that its advocates prided themselves upon their adherence to literal interpretation while issuing severe warnings against allegorical interpretation. Of course, they did not dismiss figurative meanings out of hand, but subscribed to the general principle that if the literal meaning makes good sense, then no other meaning is to be sought. That there were seven such congregations in the late first century, and that much of what was said to them was specifically based upon their local contexts, no one doubts.[6] The critical issue, then, is whether there is any indication in the text of Revelation that the seven churches refer to something beyond the local congregations and their first-century circumstances.

The logic behind the theory of church ages begins with John's statement that the purpose of the Apocalypse is to reveal things past, present, and future (Rev. 1:19). To determine what is revealed about things future, allegorical meanings are assigned to the seven churches. From there the dispensational commentators point out the parallelisms between each church's character and the character of the particular period of church history, from ancient to modern, that it represents. They also point out that the meanings of the names of the seven churches suggest these various periods. Ephesus means "beloved," so it must refer to the apostolic church. Smyrna means "bitterness," so it must refer to the period of the great persecutions. Pergamum means "thoroughly married," so it must symbolize the alliance of the church and Rome under Constantine. Thyatira means "perpetual sacrifice," so it must refer to the Roman Catholic Church which dominated the Middle Ages. And so the scheme goes.

The ingenuity of this scheme may be impressive, but its Achilles' heel is exegesis. There is nothing in the text of Revelation to warrant such an allegorical treatment. In fact some recent dispensationalists have given up on it altogether. To arbitrarily assign the seven congregations of Asia to the future begs the question, since they already existed in the late first century. Among the evidence are letters Ignatius wrote to three of the seven (Smyrna, Ephesus, and Philadelphia) in the early second century. Whether or not John intended the statement "what you have seen, what is now and what will take place later" as a paradigm for interpreting his book is moot. Even if he did, the fact that the seven congregations that received the original treatise were spread over western Asia Minor argues strongly that, if anything, they must belong to the category of "what is now," not "what will take place later." That the allegorical interpretation is unlikely is probably the most that can be said. In any case, as a schematic to deduce the approximate time of Jesus' second coming, it is entirely too subjective to be of any enduring value.

Theories Based on World Evangelism

A rather different approach is sometimes offered on the basis of Jesus' announcement, "This gospel of the kingdom will be preached in the whole world as a testimony to all nations, and then the end will come" (Matt. 24:14; Mark 13:10). When this declaration is attached to Peter's statements that the Lord has delayed his return in order to demonstrate his patience toward those who are yet to be saved (2 Peter 3:9, 15a), and that Christians can "speed" the coming of the day of God (2 Peter 3:12), then a case can be made that the Christian church can affect the timing of the end. By appealing to the great missionary endeavors of past centuries as well as current missionary efforts augmented by mass communication technologies, it can be argued that soon, for the first time in human history, every person on the globe will have heard the gospel. Though such reckoning sets no dates, its advocates suggest that the return of Christ can be expected in the very near future, perhaps within our own generation.

There are some flaws in this theory, however. First, after two thousand years of Christian missions, 67 percent of the world still is not Christian. Second, there is no scholarly consensus about the translation of 2 Peter 3:12. To be sure, several English versions render the Greek word *speudontas* as "hurrying" the day of God or some such equivalent (so NIV, RSV, NASB, TEV, NAB, KJV). Other versions, however, opt for the translation "as you wait eagerly" (RV, ASV, NEB, JB, Phillips, Weymouth, Williams), which is equally possible. Third, while modern missionary efforts are not to be discounted, Paul, at least, seemed to interpret the idea of the gospel proclaimed to the whole world in somewhat looser terms than does this theory. He had no hesitation in saying that even in the first century "all over the world this gospel is producing fruit and growing" (Col. 1:6). Furthermore, he wished to push westward to Spain, since in Palestine, Asia Minor, and Greece the gospel had already been "fully proclaimed"; indeed, "There is no more place for me to work in these regions" (Rom. 15:19, 23). To the Colossians he boldly announced, "The gospel that you heard . . . has been proclaimed to every creature under heaven" (Col. 1:23). Perhaps he meant only that the gospel had reached the major urban centers of the Roman Empire, or perhaps his statement was an oblique reference to the cross as a cosmic event "proclaimed" to the world in the sense that it was performed for the world. Regardless, Paul's statements discourage interpreting Jesus' words as narrowly as do some advocates of current missionary technologies.

Concerning Jesus' prediction, it should be pointed out that in the history of Christianity there was never a time when the gospel was universally proclaimed to all people groups. Thus, even if every living soul today hears the gospel, the fact would remain that billions of people and scores of language groups have lived and died without that privilege. Contemporary mass evangelism, even if entirely successful, will not fulfil Jesus' prediction if one takes it as encompassing the whole world geography or the sum of all the world's nations and language groups.

How, then, should one understand Jesus' words? R. T. France is probably correct when he says that Jesus' prediction refers to "an extension of the disciples' mission beyond the limits imposed in [Matt.] 10:5–6 and 15:24, and now Jesus points clearly to a time when Israel's special priority will be over."[7] A translation factor also must be considered. Both Matthew and Mark use the word *ethnoi* ("the nations, Gentiles, pagans"). Matthew also uses the word *oikoumenē* ("the inhabited earth, the Roman world"). So it is quite possible that Matthew 24:14 should be translated, "And this gospel of the kingdom will be proclaimed in all the world [i.e., the Mediterranean world] for a testimony to all the Gentiles, and then the end will come." If this is the correct meaning, the universal offer of the gospel to the nations beyond the confines of the Jewish community was accomplished long ago in the Book of Acts and the history of the early church. The prediction may have been a preliminary sign during the Jewish period of the early church, but it can hardly be one today.

Classical postmillennialists, taking a slightly different tack, believe that there will be a conversion of all nations before the Lord's return. Arguing from the prophets, the psalms, and the parables of Jesus, they expect "the salvation of an incredibly large number of the race of mankind." In the end, "the number of the redeemed shall then be swelled until it far surpasses that of the lost."[8] For the postmillennialist, however, the conclusion concerning the timing of Christ's coming is just the opposite of the premillennialist or even the amillennialist position. The postmillennialist pushes the return of Christ into the far future, centuries, and possibly even millennia, beyond the Christianization of the world. The postmillennialist thus restricts the time of the second coming so that it cannot be in the near future. Though the result is markedly different from premillennial date-setting, it is still an attempt to establish the general time of Christ's return.

Various objections to the postmillennial viewpoint have been offered. Biblically, postmillennial thought does not seem to do justice to the New Testament emphasis that the advent of Christ is to be anticipated as near. Jesus' great eschatological discourse seems to portray the worsening of spiritual and moral conditions in the world, not their alleviation (Matt. 24:9–14). Paul agrees (1 Tim. 4:1–5; 2 Tim. 3:1–5). Pragmatically, there seems to be little evidence for the Christianization of the world. The older postmillennial arguments that scientific and technological advances are signs of Christian progress are doubtful, to say the least. The two world wars, not to mention numerous atrocities since, demonstrate that human capacity for evil has not abated, in spite of almost two millennia of Christian influence in the West. The accomplishments of the League of Nations, and later the United Nations, have been modest. So the notion that the second coming of Christ is still far in the future, that the church age will be much longer than two millennia, and that the present age cannot end until there is a massive conversion of the nations to Christianity is dubious if not impossible.

In the end, there seems to be no viable method for calculating the length of the church era. It already seems to have lasted much longer than any of the apostles expected. How much longer will it last? No one knows.

What about the "Signs of the Times"?

One of the most common types of attempts to date the return of the Lord focuses on the so-called signs of the times. Signs of the times are believed to be direct correlations between historical events and biblical predictions about the end of the age. Even if one cannot calculate the length of the church age, still there may be events within history, anticipated by the biblical prophets, which signal the close of the age.

The modern approach to signs of the times goes back to the revival of millenarian thought in Europe and especially Great Britain in the early

1800s. The French Revolution had resulted in the violent uprooting of European political and social institutions, leading many to conclude that the end of the age was upon them. The destruction of papal power in France, the confiscation of church property, and the elevation of reason over religion were heralded as direct fulfilments of the prophecies about the little horn and the beast (Dan. 7; Rev. 13). In 1798 the French marched on Rome and banished the pope, an act that was interpreted as the "deadly wound" of the beast from the sea (Rev. 13:3) because it occurred exactly 1,260 years after 538, the year in which the papacy was reckoned to have first achieved peak power. The climate was right for a new passion concerning prophetic interpretation![9]

In the Church of England as well as Scottish Presbyterianism a fascination developed about the possibility of the Jews returning to Palestine. The Old Testament prophets had predicted that the people of Israel would be restored to their land. Conferences on biblical prophecy became the order of the day, the chief concerns of which were prophetic chronology, the second advent of Christ, and the restoration of the Jews. Eventually the older postmillennialism began to give way to the budding premillennialism. By 1830 the new millenarians had concluded that the restoration of the Jews to Palestine should be expected as a sign of the last days. In their view, the second advent of Christ would occur prior to the millennium, while the 1,260 years of Daniel and Revelation already had reached their terminus during the French Revolution.

In retrospect, the accuracy of these conclusions is less important than the fact that a pattern of interpretation had been established which would continue into the twentieth century. This effort to correlate biblical predictions with specific events in Western history has been alive and well ever since.

Into this mix of eschatological speculation there stepped a man whose influence would far outstrip the memory of his name, John Nelson Darby (1800–1882). Much has been written about Darby of the Plymouth Brethren movement. For our purposes it will suffice to point out that he, more than any other, popularized a system of prophetic interpretation that allowed the bulk of prophecies in Daniel and Revelation to be considered as futuristic. Traditional historicism, with its view that many of these prophecies had already been fulfilled, was on the wane. Darby asserted that almost everything was still to come. This futuristic vision, called dispensationalism, became the groundwork for modern attempts to correlate contemporary history with biblical prophecy.[10]

The ideas of dispensationalism gradually moved across the Atlantic to America. By the end of the American Civil War, supporters of the millenarian movement had reached the conclusion that they were already living in the last periods of the present dispensation. Great judgments were pending over Christendom, and Christ would soon appear. It is not without significance that the titles of the most popular prophetic periodicals were *Prophetic Times, Waymarks in the Wilderness,* and *Signs of Our Times.* As the nineteenth century drew to a close, the general belief among millenarians was that the characteristics of the age—wars, international unrest, famines, pestilences, persecutions, and false Christs—were intensifying, and this intensification was a sign that the end could be at any moment. These dispensational ideas and interpretations of signs of the times were widely disseminated through the extensive notes about prophecy that appeared in the Scofield Reference Bible.

The logic of the dispensational approach was drawn primarily from Jesus' eschatological discourse given in response to the disciples' question "What will be the sign of your coming and of the end of the age?" (Matt. 24:3). It was popularly believed that Matthew 24:4–14 serves as a description of the signs marking the close of the age. Various other signs, drawn from both the Old and the New Testaments, were added to produce a whole series of prophetic fulfilments that heralded the end.

The Sign of the Jews' Return to Palestine

One of the most important signs was the return of the Jews to Palestine. Whereas the millenarians had projected that the Jews would return to Palestine, the Zionist movement (late nineteenth and twentieth centuries) seemed to corroborate their belief. Nothing, however, could match the excitement at the end of World War II when the State of Israel was established on May 14, 1948. Had not the millenarians been predicting this very thing for over a hundred years? It seemed to be a powerful vindication of their hermeneutic!

A distinguishing mark of dispensationalism is the belief in two spiritual programs, Israel and the church. The divine election of the Jews by God as his ethnic people is inviolable. Though they may have been suspended from God's attention during the church age, God will return to them because of his unconditional covenant with Abraham. Furthermore, Palestine is Israel's inalienable earthly possession. God gave it to Abraham, Isaac, and Jacob by divine grant (Gen. 17:7–8; 26:2–3; 28:13–15). Of particular note is that the warnings of the Hebrew prophets about the scattering of Israel among the nations applied not only to the Old Testament exile, but also to the dispersion following the two Jewish revolts (A.D. 66–73 and 135). Now inasmuch as this prophetic dispersion of the Jews was a New Testament phenomenon, the regathering of the Jews should also be taken as futuristic rather than as something fulfilled in the Old Testament return of the exiles under Zerubba-bel (Amos 9:14–15). Thus, when the Zionist Jews began filtering back to Palestine, and especially when a national State of Israel was formed in 1948, the dispensationalists argued that Old Testament predictions were being directly fulfilled, a clear sign of the end of the age.

Even more to the point, a number of interpreters saw in Jesus' para-ble of the blossoming fig tree a perfect analogy of the Jews' restoration to Palestine (Matt. 24:32–35). The fig tree, they argued, is a symbol of the nation Israel. Hal Lindsey wrote, "When the Jewish people, after nearly 2,000 years of exile under relentless persecution, became a nation again on 14 May 1948, the 'fig tree' put forth its first leaves." Further-more, pointing to Jesus' additional comment that "this generation will not pass until all is fulfilled" and reckoning that a biblical generation was about forty years, Lindsey and others boldly announced that "within forty years or so of 1948" Jesus would return.[11] They also took note of Jesus' statement that Jerusalem would be trampled by the Gentiles until the times of the Gentiles were fulfilled (Luke 21:24); with the establishment of the State of Israel and Jews flooding back to the Holy Land, the Gen-tile period might well be nearly over!

The Signs of Natural Disasters and Political Turmoil

The establishment of the State of Israel was only one among several important signs of the times, however. The proliferation of natural dis-asters seemed to parallel Jesus' warnings of famines, earthquakes, and pestilences. The repeated outbreak of war, including World Wars I and II, the Cold War, the Korean War, the Vietnam War, and a host of smaller conflicts, seemed to parallel Jesus' prediction that "nation will rise against nation" (Matt. 24:7). The technological revolution seemed to bear out in a remarkable way the prophet Daniel's prediction that "knowledge shall be increased" (Dan. 12:4 KJV). The depiction in Revelation of the beast's compelling everyone to have a qualifying mark on the hand or forehead in order to buy and sell (Rev. 13:16–17) suggested that the world should expect the rise of some sort of universal economic system; computerization, international bar codes, subcutaneous microchips, and the like combined to send shivers of excitement among the faithful. And the triumph of liberal Christianity in the fundamentalist wars of the early twentieth century was surely the fulfilment of Paul's prediction about the great falling away (2 Thess. 2:3 KJV).

Two other world political events seemed to dovetail perfectly into the collage of apocalyptic signs. One was the threat of communism from the Soviet Union and China. Ezekiel had predicted an invasion of Palestine from the north, and Hal Lindsey popularized the hypothesis that the Hebrew words *Rosh* and *Meshech* (Ezek. 38:2–3) bear a direct linguistic connection to the modern names Russia and Moscow. The Apocalypse of John described a terrible war in which an army of 200 million troops, coming from the east, would annihilate a third of the earth's population (Rev. 9:13–16; 16:12). Had not the Chinese Communists boasted that they could field a militia just that large? Fueled by the anxieties of the Cold War, anticipation of a Communist offensive against the relatively new State of Israel seemed plausible.

The other great political event was the formation of the European Common Market (now the European Union). In 1958 a number of European nations established a common market or tariff union. By the mid-1970s most of the major Western European nations, including Britain, France, and West Germany, were members. Speculation ran wild that this economic bloc might be the confederation of kingdoms predicted by Daniel (Dan. 2:41–43; 7:7b, 24) and John (Rev. 13:1; 17:12–13). Daniel had said, "In the time of those kings, the God of heaven will set up a kingdom that will never be destroyed" (Dan. 2:44), and "the kingdoms under the whole heaven will be handed over to the saints, the people of the Most High" (Dan. 7:27). John had said that these same kings would "make war against the Lamb" (Rev. 17:14). Might the establishment of the European Union be the prelude to Armageddon and the millennial reign of Jesus Christ? Might this European Union be the revival of the ancient Roman Empire which had persecuted the early church and now been healed of its death wound (Rev. 13:3)?

The cumulative effect of these interpretations was convincing to some people, for the whole seemed greater than the sum of its parts. Some might argue about this sign or that—some might disagree about this interpretation or that—but minor disagreements aside, the cumulative impression was strong that the last quarter of the twentieth century might well be the curtain call of history. The moving scene of ultraorthodox Jews praying every hour at the western wall of the temple mount in Jerusalem, and the rumors of their plans to build yet another temple, were like the rumblings of distant thunder. To be sure, Jesus said that no one knows the day or hour of his return (Matt. 24:36), but did he not also say, "When you see these things happening, you know that the kingdom of God is near" (Luke 21:31)? Did not Paul imply that such signs were obvious indications of the nearness of the Lord's return (1 Thess. 5:1)?

As we turn to an assessment of these interpretations, the reader should bear in mind that Jesus in fact did urge his disciples to watch for his return (Matt. 24:42; 25:13; Mark 13:32–37; Luke 12:35–40). Furthermore, he urged the disciples, "When these things begin to take place, stand up and lift up your heads, because your redemption is drawing near" (Luke 21:28). At the same time *it must also be pointed out that Jesus discouraged speculation.* When the disciples, curious about the time of Jerusalem's destruction, asked, "When will these things happen?" Jesus responded, "Watch out that you are not deceived. For many will come in my name, claiming, 'I am he,' and 'The time is near.' Do not follow them. When you hear of wars and revolutions, do not be frightened. These things must happen first, but the end will not come right away" (Luke 21:8–9).

Perhaps the single most important point to be made concerning Jesus' admonition to "watch" is the context surrounding his imperative. Jesus instructed his followers to watch, not so they could figure out the time of his return, but so they would not be caught unawares when it happened. Readiness, not the date on the calendar, was the clear focus of Jesus' words. Quite plainly Jesus told his disciples that no one, not even the angels and not even the Son of God himself, knows the time of the second advent. Only God the Father knows (Matt. 24:36, 42; 25:13; Mark 13:32, 35)! Is it not presumptuous to attempt to discover something Jesus said no one could possibly know? It was not the expectedness, but the unexpectedness of his second advent that Jesus emphasized.

The parables that Jesus gave to illustrate this unexpectedness are particularly forceful. His second advent would be as sudden as the great deluge (Matt. 24:36–41), as unexpected as a burglary (Matt. 24:42–44), as startling as the unanticipated return of a traveling estate-owner (Matt. 24:45–51), and as abrupt as the nocturnal arrival of a Jewish groom to take his bride home (Matt. 25:1–13). None of these parables give the slightest indication that the time of the event could be calculated. Rather, they pointedly suggest the opposite. The disciples were to watch because they did not know when the great event would take place.

It is well known, of course, that the form of Jesus' eschatological discourse is not identical in the Synoptic Gospels. The problems associated with harmonizing the three accounts are much too complex to treat here, but most agree the sermon was prompted by the disciples' question about the destruction of Herod's temple. In the discourse Jesus begins by addressing the coming destruction of Jerusalem and ends by talking about his second coming at the end of the age. Interpreters wrestle with where in the text the transition takes place between the two topics. Some believe that they are superimposed upon each other and cannot be separated. Others suggest that the focus of the first part of the discourse is entirely on the destruction of Jerusalem (Matt. 24:4–35; Mark 13:5–31; Luke 21:8–33), while comments on the parousia occur only at the end (Matt. 24:36–25:46; Mark 13:32–37; Luke 21:34–36). Still others regard the majority of the discourse as referring to the parousia, excepting only Luke 21:12–24.

Regardless of the differences in all three versions, a constant theme is the suppression of speculation. Mark's version is instructive. Though the discourse certainly describes a number of future events as precursors to the end of history, Jesus deliberately sought to curtail speculation. "Watch out that no one deceives you," Jesus counseled (Mark 13:5). Traumatic events like wars would certainly happen, but the disciples were not to take them as anything other than the beginning of birth pangs, certainly not as signs of the consummation (Mark 13:7–8). Persecutions would accompany their missionary efforts, but such opposition was only to be expected (Mark 13:9–13). Some would announce the coming of the Messiah, but the faithful were to ignore such reports (Mark 13:21–23). One must conclude that Jesus' primary purpose here was to issue a strong warning against misunderstanding penultimate events as though they were final ones.

Jesus' warning puts the so-called signs of the times in a very different light! Traumatic events will characterize the age, but they are not compass points by which to plot the end of time. To be sure, some have countered that while no one knows the day or hour, Christians should be able to plot the times and seasons (1 Thess. 5:1). This misses entirely Paul's point, for when Paul writes that he does not need to discuss times and dates, he does so because the time of Christ's coming is unknown (1 Thess. 5:2–3). The only reason that the return of the Lord will not break upon Christians as a surprise is that they are constantly expecting it (1 Thess. 5:4–11). To expect something is not at all the same thing as predicting when it will happen.

So how valid is the hermeneutic of using the signs of the times to predict the time of Christ's return? Without dismissing it out of hand, we should note some significant weaknesses in its case. Even something as politically significant as Zionism and the establishment of the State of Israel is less than a clear signal. For there is no Christian consensus that ethnic Jews in the twentieth century are the heirs to the promises of the Hebrew prophets. If, as Peter said nearly two millennia ago, "God fulfilled what he had foretold through all the prophets" (Acts 3:18), and "All the prophets from Samuel on, as many as have spoken, have foretold these days [i.e., the rise of the Christian church]" (Acts 3:24), then the fulfilment of the Old Testament predictions occurred primarily in the life of Jesus and the Christian church. Christians are the spiritual heirs of ancient Israel. Peter boldly proclaimed to his listeners in Jerusalem who heard the message about Jesus, "You are heirs of the prophets and of the covenant God made with your fathers" (Acts 3:25). The dynasty of David has been restored, not in Palestine, but in Jesus the Messiah, the "Root and Offspring of David" who reigns over the whole universe (Rev. 22:16; 2 Tim. 2:8).

In the previous chapter we discussed the dawn of the time of fulfillment at length. If the conclusions drawn there are valid, then the idea is doubtful that the Jews must return to Palestine in order to preserve the integrity of Old Testament prophecy. If the seed of Abraham is to be defined by faith rather than pedigree (Gal. 3:7–9, 29; Rom. 4:9–12, 16–17, 22–24; 9:6–8), and if true Jewishness is primarily a spiritual, not a genealogical matter (Rom. 2:28–29; Heb. 6:13–20), and if Christians are now "the chosen" and "the diaspora" (1 Peter 1:1–2, 17; 2:11), and, finally, if the land grant of Canaan is ultimately fulfilled, not in the eastern Mediterranean, but in the Christian inheritance of heaven which "can never perish, spoil or fade" (1 Peter 1:4; Gal. 4:26; Heb. 12:22–23), then the notion that the Jews must return to Palestine is hardly a compelling one.

To be sure, Christians must never put God in a box, telling him what he cannot do. We cannot rule out the possibility that God may have some purpose in the modern return of the Jews to Palestine and the establishment of the State of Israel. A critical passage in this regard is Paul's discussion in Romans 11. What does Paul mean when he asserts, "Did God reject his people? By no means!" (Rom. 11:1)? Similarly, what does he have in mind when he affirms, "So all Israel will be saved!" (Rom. 11:26)? Dispensationalists usually take "Israel" to refer to modern Jews who will be converted to Christianity during the great tribulation. The amillennialist says "Israel" is to be taken in a spiritual sense; thus the term includes both Jews and Gentiles who have faith in Christ. Still others conclude that "Israel" here refers to those Jews who have been converted to Christianity throughout the entire church age. The lack of exegetical clarity on this passage should discourage dogmatism. As George Ladd pointed out, "The New Testament sheds no light on this problem."[12] Still, the possibility that God may have a plan for the Jewish people as a group should not be lightly dismissed.

Hal Lindsey's popular interpretation that Jesus' analogy of the fig tree is a symbol of the restoration of the State of Israel must be regarded as unsound. For there is no historical evidence suggesting that the fig tree was a recognized symbol of the Jewish nation in the first century. Since nothing in the context of Jesus' discourse suggests such symbolism, the interpretation must be rejected. More to the point, Jesus compared the fig tree's spring growth of twigs and leaves to "all these things," not to one particular thing (Matt. 24:32–33). And Luke extends Jesus' analogy to "all the trees" (Luke 21:29), a comparison that could hardly have any specificity regarding the establishment of the State of Israel in 1948!

In regard to other so-called signs, such as a possible Russian-Chinese invasion of Israel and the establishment of the European Union, it must be said that speculation in this area is doubtful, and in some cases based on outright exegetical blunders. A Communist invasion by Russia and China seemed quite plausible during the Cold War, but with the tremendous political changes in Eastern Europe and Russia, the idea is no longer realistic. Exegetically, the attempt to extract the names "Russia" and "Moscow" out of *Rosh* and *Meshech* in Ezekiel 38:2–3 is dubious, to say the least. It is always hazardous to attempt a firm connection between ancient people groups and modern nations, if for no other reason than intervening migrations. True, English versions of the Bible are split over whether the Hebrew term *Rosh* is simply the common word for "chief" (so NIV, RSV, NAB, KJV) or a place name (so RV, NEB, NASB, ASV, NKJV). Even if it is a place name, however, an appeal to etymology based on similarity of sound is not linguistically valid. It is one thing to point out that the Hebrew word *Rosh* sounds similar to the word "Russia," but such a similarity in no way proves a linguistic connection. The same sort of nebulous argument was used in the Anglo-Israel theology of the British Empire's heyday to prove that the Anglo-Saxons were the so-called lost ten tribes of Israel: because the Hebrew word for covenant, *běrît,* sounds like "Brit," the true covenant people must be the British. Serious students of the Bible will avoid such nonsense. Similar reservations must be extended to the talk about a revived Roman Empire in modern Europe. The prediction of ten kingdoms allied with the Antichrist is certainly a feature of biblical prophecy (Dan. 7:24; Rev. 17:12), but the biblical information is too scant to make any firm connection with the European Union.

What, then, should be the Christian position with regard to "the signs of the times"? Should we try to correlate modern political events with biblical prophecies in an effort to predict the time of Jesus' return? The fact that, so far, every attempt has failed should discourage anyone from saying yes. The ambiguities of biblical prophecy have become the kingpin in the speculative machine. More often than not, attempts to calculate the moment of the end say more about the ingenuity of the interpreter than the message of the Bible. The teachings of Jesus urge Christians to view the signs of the times as motivations toward watchfulness, not invitations to speculation! Jesus said to the Twelve, "What I say to you, I say to everyone: 'Watch!'" (Mark 13:37).

Why Christians Should Be Wary of Speculation

The New Testament declares that the return of Christ is "near" and "soon" (Rom. 13:11–12; Phil. 4:5; James 5:7–9; Rev. 2:16; 3:11; 22:7, 12, 20). Such ambiguous language is entirely to be expected if, as Jesus plainly stated, the time of his coming is unknown (Matt. 24:36–51; Mark 13:32–37; Luke 21:29–36). However, there is a further issue that should be considered. It might well be that the ambiguity of New Testament language is intended precisely to discourage speculation. If such ambiguity is intentional, not merely incidental, then the attempt to calculate the time of Jesus' return is not a harmless diversion. It is an effort directly opposing the theology of Scripture. To be sure, Christians must not lapse into lethargy concerning the return of Christ, but neither should they entangle themselves in a perpetual motion–machine of calendar speculation. Such speculation appeals to the same human curiosity that fuels interest in the occult, New Age philosophy, and other thought forms that attempt to tap into sources of hidden knowledge. The Bible, far from being revered as God's redemptive revelation of himself in Jesus Christ, becomes a cryptic source book by which to predict the future. Prophetic study becomes a temptation toward the sensational.

Since many if not most of the biblical passages about the last days appear in an apocalyptic context, especially the books of Daniel and Revelation, it is important to take into account the apocalyptic genre when interpreting these passages. Failure to do so may well be the most serious error of the current spate of end-time prognosticators. Apocalyptic is full of literary symbols, and, as Grant Osborne has well stated, "The task of the interpreter is to determine which figurative sense the symbol has in the larger context. This means that the true meaning is not to be found in our present situation but rather in the use of that symbol in its ancient setting. This point can hardly be overemphasized in light of the misuse of biblical symbols in many circles today."[13] There is a cultural gap between the present and the past. The symbols in the Book of Revelation, for instance, originated in ancient Jewish culture as well as Greco-Roman culture. Similarly, symbols in the Old Testament prophets must be interpreted against the background of the ancient Near East. Modern Christians who attempt to interpret ancient texts without regard for the genre or the ancient culture in which those texts arose are almost certain to go astray.

It is also well to bear in mind what Jesus said about sign seeking: "A wicked and adulterous generation looks for a miraculous sign" (Matt. 16:4). Jesus taught that the kingdom of God does not come visibly, as though its arrival could be pointed out by acclamations of "Here it is" or "There it is." In fact, he warned against people who make such claims: "Do not go running after them. For the Son of Man in his day will be like the lightning, which flashes and lights up the sky from one end to the other" (Luke 17:20–24).

Another reason that Christians should be wary of speculation is quite practical. Failed prognostications have taken a heavy toll, both emotionally and financially, on the faith of many sincere people. Not only have they lost faith in the prognosticators, they have often lost faith in the Word of God and the blessed hope of the church. Those who attempt to predict the future should be more sensitive to the aftermath of their failures. Without doubt, they shall be accountable in the great judgment, where every idle word will be examined.

Finally, Christians should be wary of speculation precisely because of their human limitations. Theological humility, not arrogance, should be the order of the day. Concerning the future Paul candidly admitted that "we see but a poor reflection," and in the present we "know [only] in part" (1 Cor. 13:12). What is wrong with frankly accepting such limitations?

A pertinent example of human limitation is the failure of the rabbis and the Jewish constituency in general to recognize Jesus as the Messiah. Because they were hardened in their own interpretive methodologies, they were closed to God's greatest act in history, the sending of his Son! This is not to say that theology and interpretation are unimportant, but the failure of biblical students in the first century should lead us toward less dogmatism about fixing the meanings of prophecies before God fulfils them. Even though the Jewish thinkers diligently studied the Scriptures, they still refused to acknowledge Jesus (John 5:39–40)!

It is well to remember that God sovereignly chooses how the words of his prophets will be fulfilled. God alone manages history. Sometimes what may seem to be a simple prediction is actually much more complex than one might suppose. Take, for example, Malachi's prediction that before the coming of the day of the Lord, Elijah the prophet would appear (Mal. 4:5–6). The plain, straightforward meaning of the prediction led the rabbis to expect the personal return of Elijah. In fact, even today at the Jewish Passover meal, a place is ceremonially reserved for Elijah. A cup of wine is filled and set in the middle of the table should Elijah come to the home that night.

In like manner, when John the Baptizer preached in the desert, the temple authorities sent a delegation to ask him point-blank if he were Elijah (John 1:21). John answered bluntly, "I am not!" Later, others speculated that Jesus might be Elijah (Matt. 16:14; Mark 6:15; 8:28; Luke 9:8, 19). Such notions were grounded in the expectation of a literal fulfilment of Malachi's words. However, in spite of John's disclaimer, Jesus pointedly indicated that John was "the Elijah who was to come" (Matt. 11:14; 17:10–13). Did John fulfil the prediction about Elijah? Jesus apparently thought so, even if John did not! In addition, the angel had declared to Zechariah that John's ministry would be carried out "in the spirit and power of Elijah" (Luke 1:17).

The point here is not to use the Elijah prediction as a paradigm for interpreting prophecy, but to demonstrate that God fulfils his own prophecies, sometimes in unexpected ways. That God does so suggests that Christians should be reserved about too confidently putting forth their various theories concerning the time of Christ's return. One professor had it right when he advised his students, "Draw all your prophecy charts on cheap paper—then it won't be so hard to tear them up!" In the end, the question "Should Christians try to predict Christ's return?" must be answered with a respectful no.

What Must Christians Believe about the Last Days?

As mentioned at the outset, the systems of prophetic interpretation, even among evangelicals, are widely divergent. Which one is right—or is any of them right? How do the prophetic interpretive systems influence the way their adherents read particular biblical passages about the end times, and conversely, how does their exegesis of such passages shape the different ideologies they hold? These are the kinds of issues addressed in this chapter. Our approach will be to survey the basic systems, the basic theological questions they generate, and the way each system handles key biblical passages. In the end, we will offer an assessment as to the importance of such systems to the evangelical faith.

We begin with the central event. The central event in eschatology, other than the first coming of Jesus Christ, is his second coming. Theologians treat the second coming in remarkably different ways, but it remains the touchstone of all eschatology. There are three primary New Testament words that denote Christ's second coming:

parousia = the presence, arrival, or coming of Christ
epiphaneia = the manifestation or appearing of Christ
apokalypsis = the revelation or disclosure of Christ

These three words seem to be used more or less interchangeably to denote the second advent. Jesus said the *parousia* of the Son of man would be like lightning (Matt. 24:27). Paul speaks of the *"epiphany* of Christ's *parousia"* (2 Thess. 2:8), the *"parousia* of our Lord Jesus with all his saints" (1 Thess. 3:13), and the *"epiphany* of the glory of our great God and Savior" (Titus 2:13). He also says the church waits for the *apocalypse* of our Lord Jesus Christ (1 Cor. 1:7). At the *apocalypse* the enemies of God will be paid back while the church will be relieved (2 Thess. 1:6–7). Paul therefore exhorts the church to maintain its Christian lifestyle until the *"epiphany* of our Lord Jesus Christ" (1 Tim. 6:14; 2 Tim. 4:8). Peter also speaks of the believers' honor and perfection at the *"apocalypse* of Jesus Christ" (1 Peter 1:7, 13; 4:13).

In general, the evangelical emphasis is that Jesus' second coming will be personal, visible, and literal. That emphasis distinguishes evangelical theology(ies) from the modern theologies. Realized and existential eschatology, for instance, propose either that the second coming was fulfilled in the descent of the Holy Spirit (i.e., is not personal), is currently fulfilled in an existential encounter with Christ (i.e., is not visible), or will be fulfilled in the union of the believer's spirit with Christ at the moment of death (i.e., is not literal). But even among evangelicals who agree that Christ's return will be personal, visible, and literal, there is considerable variation of opinion about the surrounding events. Most of these opinions fit into one or another of the various eschatological systems.

Eschatological systems are structures superimposed upon the data of the Bible. By definition they seek to establish coherence, logic, and plausibility while addressing the various questions that the study of eschatology raises. It is the nature of systems to seek inner consistency. Incongruities are harmonized, discrepancies are rationalized, and the loose ends are tucked in. It is fair to say that the most recent eschatological systems owe much to our fascination with Western rationalism. It is only natural that centuries of theological study have led today to various systems, each seeking to comprehend all the threads of eschatology and weave them into a self-consistent tapestry of the end times.

The Basic Systems

There are three primary evangelical approaches to the study of eschatology: covenant theology, dispensationalism, and salvation-history. Until the nineteenth century, covenant theology was clearly dominant; dispensationalism was unknown. By the early twentieth century, dispensationalism had become dominant, at least in fundamentalist American

Protestantism, and remains so today. Less well known, except among scholars, is salvation-history, a broader interpretive approach arising directly out of the modern revival of biblical theology.

Covenant Theology

Covenant theology has roots in the Reformation (sixteenth century) and post-Reformation (seventeenth and eighteenth centuries) eras. Ulrich Zwingli and Heinrich Bullinger developed it; John Calvin and other Reformers embraced it. Throughout the next several generations Protestants continued to develop and refine the tenets of covenant theology so that it became dominant in the Calvinist churches. Though opposed by Lutherans (because in their view it failed to take sufficient account of the law-gospel structure of Scripture), and later by dispensationalists (because in their view it confused the various dispensations and the Israel/church dichotomy), covenant theology continued to spread from Switzerland to Germany to the Netherlands to the British Isles and on to America. It reached its highest expression in English Puritanism in the last half of the seventeenth century and was taken up into the Westminster Confession.

The thesis of covenant theology is that all biblical theology is to be systematically arranged around the notion of covenant, particularly with respect to redemption, works, and grace. The covenant of redemption is the foundational covenant. It was entered into by God with Jesus Christ, who as the second Adam (as opposed to the created Adam) is a spiritual representative of the human race. In consideration of Jesus' perfect obedience and sacrificial death, God resolved to grant forgiveness and give eternal life to humans. Before the foundation of the world, the covenant of redemption was made between God the Father and God the Son, the Father appointing the Son to be the second Adam and mediator of the covenant, and the Son accepting this commission. Thus God guaranteed that his creation would not be destroyed by sin and that human rebellion would be overcome by grace. Christ would be the new head of humanity, the Savior of the world, and God the Father would be glorified. This covenant in its essence foresaw the inevitability of human sin and established a countermeasure.

The covenant of works, also called the old covenant, was entered into by God with Adam, the federal head of the human race, who was created as a free creature with knowledge, righteousness, and holiness. It was a covenant demanding absolute obedience for a probationary period. If Adam met the stipulations laid down in Eden about the tree of the knowledge of good and evil, God promised to grant eternal life to the human race through Adam. Adam and the race would then have passed into a state where they would have been unable to sin, whereas before, although Adam was righteous, he was free to sin. If the conditions were not met, then the threat of death remained. Adam, of course, failed to keep the conditions, a failure that resulted in the fall of humankind. Adam acted representatively for the human race. The penalty of death was executed upon all of Adam's race, and Adam's descendants are now born in sin. Apart from God's special intervention, there would be no hope at all; all would be lost forever.

The covenant of works continues to play a role in God's redemptive plan even after the fall of Adam. As expressions of this covenant, Mosaic law and especially the Ten Commandments are intended to continually convince humans of the necessity of obedience, the sinfulness of sin, the depravity of the race, and their essential need for Christ.

The covenant of grace, also called the new covenant, was made between God and the elect. In it God offers life and salvation through Jesus Christ to all who believe the gospel. Humans are hopelessly estranged from God. All are lost, but by God's grace some were chosen to be saved. Faith, which is itself God's gift to the elect, is the sole condition of the covenant of grace for both Old Testament and New Testament believers.

Covenant theology is obviously compatible with the five points of Calvinism: total depravity, unconditional election, limited atonement, irresistible grace, and perseverance. Moreover, in some ways similar to dispensationalists, covenant theologians frequently divide history into distinctive eras, such as the eras from Adam to Abraham, Abraham to Moses, Moses to Christ, Jesus' birth to resurrection, Jesus' resurrection to his parousia, and Jesus' parousia to the consummation of God's eternal purpose. In all these various eras of history the people of God are those who are elect. Distinctive eras notwithstanding, covenant theologians do not accept the dispensational dichotomy of Israel and the church. Instead, they see unity and continuity in the covenant of grace, even though in Jesus Christ there are gifts available that were unknown in earlier periods. It is this essential continuity uniting the people of God in both Old and New Testaments that distinguishes covenant theology from dispensationalism. Whereas the dispensationalist sees two peoples of God, covenant theologians see only one.

Covenant theologians have great flexibility in eschatology. They may be either premillennial, amillennial, or postmillennial without upsetting the basic covenantal system, though they tend to be amillennial or postmillennial. The few who are premillennial do not share the dispensationalist view that the millennium will have a Jewish character. Similarly, covenant theologians do not foresee a pretribulation rapture, since they do not view Israel and the church as two separate redemptive programs. They usually regard the Old Testament covenants of Abraham and David as largely fulfilled in a spiritual way to the church. Thus covenant theologians do not look for a future redemptive program for national Israel apart from the church.

Dispensationalism

Dispensationalism, an alternative to covenant theology, originated as a protest against perceived extremes in Anglican theology.[1] Toward the beginning of the nineteenth century, a conservative reaction began in England against the popular postmillennialism of Daniel Whitby (1638–1726) and its de-emphasized doctrine of Jesus' second coming. This reaction was fueled by prophetic periodicals and prophetic conferences, and developed into a major alternative to covenant theology. While the advocates of the new system still held to the historicism typical of the Reformation (e.g., the belief that the papacy is the Antichrist), the premillennial and personal return of Christ was given renewed emphasis.

At the prophetic conferences of the times, two futuristic interpretations began to make inroads into the traditional territory of historicism. One of these interpretations, historic premillennialism, was a return to the general viewpoint of the postapostolic fathers (hence "historic"). It promoted such themes as a personal Antichrist at the end of the age, a severe tribulation followed by the second advent of Christ, and the establishment of Christ's millennial kingdom on earth. The other futuristic interpretation, dispensationalism, developed from the theological studies of John Nelson Darby of the Plymouth Brethren. A modification of historic premillennialism, it held that the second advent of Christ would occur in two stages, the first before the tribulation, when Christ would take his church to heaven, and the second at the end of the tribulation, when Christ would return in glory to establish his millennial kingdom. Most of the early premillennialists were either historicists or historic premillennialists. However, dispensationalism began to gain adherents.

A similar scenario took place in America. Whitby's postmillennialism was popular in the early nineteenth century. (It had been adopted by Jonathan Edwards of colonial fame.) Then a reaction set in. Prophetic periodicals were published, and prophetic conferences were convened. Darby visited America six times between 1859 and 1874 to preach. His dispensationalism was eagerly adopted by many. Alongside the growing popularity of dispensationalism was a dissent from those who espoused historic premillennialism or historicism. Some of them disavowed dispensationalism from the beginning. Others embraced dispensationalism in the early days only to reject it later. Thus two forms of premillennialism have come down to us, though the more popular has been dispensationalism. By the middle of the twentieth century, many conservative Protestants reared in the tradition of the Scofield Reference Bible were unaware of any eschatological position other than dispensationalism; those who were aware of other approaches viewed them with grave suspicions or as capitulations to liberalism.

Keeping in mind that no system of thought is without some variations, we can summarize the primary theological emphases of dispensationalism. A dispensation (according to C. I. Scofield, whose definition is the most traditional) is a "period of time during which man is tested in respect of obedience to some specific revelation of the will of God."[2] Each period is marked by some change in God's redemptive action; each dispensation is a new test of the "natural man" and ends in judgment. Literalism is the basic hermeneutic. A primary example is that the promises of land to Abraham and David are interpreted literally and applied futuristically. Another hermeneutical principle falls under the rubric "rightly dividing the word of truth."[3] The divisions of Scripture must be carefully noted. The schematic of the ages usually entails seven dispensations, though some later dispensationalists, like Charles Ryrie, opt for only three. All agree that the most important dispensations are law, grace, and the millennial kingdom.

Most important, dispensationalism draws a dichotomy between Israel and the church. God has two redemptive programs that are always separate in biblical history. Israel was removed from God's redemptive program before the church could be formed; similarly, the church must be raptured prior to God's returning redemptively to Israel. Consequently, the Christian church is viewed as an interruption in God's redemptive program for Israel. Not having been revealed in previous ages, the church is a mystery, and the period of the church is a parenthesis. The key to prophetic interpretation, then, is primarily Israel and secondarily the church. For the redemptive promises were made to Israel, and the church participates by virtue of Israel's rejection of Christ.

According to the dispensationalist, the millennium has a marked Jewish character. The Davidic monarchy will be restored, and the promises of land that were made to Abraham and David will be literally fulfilled. A millennial temple will be built in which the Old Testament system of blood sacrifice will be revived; the purpose of this sacrificial system will, however, be commemoration rather than atonement. Saved Gentiles will enjoy the millennial blessings under the universal rule of the Davidic monarchy. This millennial kingdom was fully offered to Israel in the first advent of Christ, an offer detailed most fully in Matthew's Gospel. Upon Israel's rejection, the kingdom was postponed to the future when God shall again redemptively turn to the Jewish people. The redemptive program of the church became a possibility through Israel's rejection of the first millennial offer, and Israel was temporarily suspended from God's redemptive action.

The Book of Daniel, and especially his prophecy of the seventy weeks, is a crucial key to dispensationalist interpretation. The first sixty-nine weeks cover the period between the return of the Jews from Babylonian exile and the coming of Christ. After the sixty-ninth week the church age occurs as a parenthesis. Finally, the seventieth week, which is the period of the great tribulation, will be completed after the rapture of the church.

Easily the most recognizable feature of dispensationalism is its commitment to a pretribulation rapture, which is a theological necessity to maintain the soteriological distinction between Israel and the church. In certain key New Testament passages the phrase "wrath of God" is interpreted to refer to the great tribulation. Having been promised exemption from God's wrath, the church will not undergo that period of affliction. In addition, the imminence of the second advent is interpreted not as a general reference to the impending second coming and surrounding events, but in the specific sense of a secret rapture at any moment. The next redemptive act by God will be the taking of the church to heaven. The second coming of Christ will occur in two phases separated by a seven-year period (Daniel's seventieth week). The first phase will be Christ's coming "for" his saints (the secret rapture of the church). The second phase will be Christ's coming "with" his saints (the visible return of Christ in glory accompanied by his church).

The closing period of terrible affliction relates specifically to God's first people, Israel. It is a seven-year period in which, after the church is removed from the world, God once more will turn redemptively to Israel. Chapters 6–19 of the Book of Revelation are interpreted in terms of Israel, not the church. And thus it is believed that the gospel of the kingdom (not necessarily the gospel of grace) will be preached by 144,000 Jewish evangelists to the entire world (Rev. 7:4; 14:1–3). In the end, the New Jerusalem will be the home of the Christian church. This holy city of Revelation 21 will be a literal, physical place to be inhabited by the people of God eternally.

Finally, we should note that from the time of Darby various dispensationalists have held the view that Christendom at large is apostate. Accordingly, the system of dispensationalism sometimes is used as a test of theological orthodoxy by its adherents.

Salvation-History

Yet a third system exists among evangelicals, salvation-history. Salvation-history, also called *Heilsgeschichte* (two combined German words meaning "salvation history" or "holy history"), is both old and new. It is a relatively modern phenomenon, at least by the name "salvation-history." However, the idea played an important role in early Christian theology, especially in the writings of Irenaeus (ca. 130–200) and Augustine (354–430), because it provided a philosophy of history. While the Greeks tended to view history as meaningless and the Romans tended to see it only in terms of their own civilization, Christian thinkers argued that history has a theological meaning quite apart from any particular human civilization. Although largely lost in medieval theology, this emphasis was revived by some Reformers, especially in connection with their interest in biblical theology. J. A. Bengel (1687–1752) is regarded as the modern father of the approach, which Jonathan Edwards adopted in his posthumous *History of Redemption*.

However, biblical theology, and with it salvation-history, was largely overshadowed by the study of dogmatics in post-Reformation scholarship. The theology of the Reformers was classified and analyzed in the less flexible categories of systematic theology. The study of Scripture was conducted under the rubrics of various philosophical categories such as prolegomena (revelation), theology (divine nature), bibliology (the inspiration and authority of Scripture), anthropology (human nature), hamartiology (the doctrine of sin), Christology (the question of Christ's natures), pneumatology (the work of the Spirit), soteriology (salvation), ecclesiology (the church), angelology, demonology, and eschatology (the last things). Finally, however, with the renewed interest in biblical theology in the early twentieth century, salvation-history came into its own. It is held today by many evangelicals throughout the world.

Salvation-history, as might be expected given its emphasis on biblical theology, takes a more organic approach to the Bible than is thought to be found in either dispensationalism or covenant theology. It is at once both harder and easier to describe than the other schematics, harder in that its fluidity makes it more difficult to categorize, and easier in that its arising out of biblical theology makes it less dependent on philosophical categories and Greek logic. In general, those who embrace salvation-history tend to view both dispensationalism and covenant theology as too artificial. They often regard as an abuse of Scripture the gathering of proof texts as raw data for systematic theology. Instead, the concern of those who embrace salvation-history is to allow the text to speak for itself so that what is central for the biblical text becomes central for the schematic, and what is secondary to the biblical text becomes secondary for the schematic.

History is the keystone of the salvation-history school, for biblical faith is first of all a historical faith. The salvation-history theologian emphasizes events that are both a part of history and, at the same time, mighty acts of God. This means that scientific historiography is unable to discern the meaning of history without the Bible's authoritative interpretation. The sacredness of a historical event is not necessarily self-evident, but is proclaimed by the Word of God. To make history central also means that the salvation-history theologian stands opposed to the theological methodologies of existentialism, mysticism, and Platonism. It is in sacred history that God has revealed himself, and the Bible is the divine record and divine interpretation of that history.

The theological midpoint of history is the Christ event. All biblical history flows toward or from this center. Biblical history is linear, not cyclical. Unlike Judaism, which placed the midpoint of time between the present age and the coming age so that the midpoint was always future, salvation-history, as a Christian theology, places the midpoint in the past, in the life, death, and resurrection of Jesus. Still, the old dividing point of Judaism retains a validity in that the future age has already impinged upon the present age. The future age in some sense began with the first advent of Christ, but the present age will not end until the second advent of Christ. Thus there is a tension between the present and the future.

Generally speaking, those who hold to salvation-history are more open to critical studies than are either dispensationalists or covenant theologians.[4] Archaeology, the study of the history and culture surrounding the biblical narratives, and literary criticism (with deference to the authority and infallibility of Scripture) are primary tools used in the work of biblical theology. Because the Greek notions of formal logic (definitions, the classification of data, deductive reasoning) were relatively late in reaching the Jewish world, the Bible is written in a Hebrew mind-set that does not flinch at paradox. The tensions between divine sovereignty and human freedom and other such problems that systematic theologians have taken upon themselves to try to resolve are allowed to remain in tension in salvation-history. If such tensions were not problematic for the original authors of Scripture, they need not be resolved today, only described.

Salvation-history gives great emphasis to placing each biblical document, as closely as possible, in its historical-cultural setting and exploring how this setting may have shaped the document. In interpretation the literary genre of the document is accorded great significance so that the document is read sympathetically and as closely as possible to the way it was intended to be read by its first readers. Reading the Bible in a "flat" way, that is, without regard for literary style, is especially to be avoided.

Salvation-history sees grace and faith as the central realities of God's redemptive action in history, whether Old Testament or New Testament. It also sees history as much less categorical than does either dispensationalism or covenant theology. It affirms progressive revelation, but not in tightly defined eras. Also, salvation-history sees the people of God in both continuity and discontinuity between the Testaments. There is discontinuity in that Christians are not in a covenantal relationship to Yahweh in the same way as was national Israel. There is continuity in that both the Old Testament and New Testament people of faith are redemptively joined together in the cross and the resurrection of Jesus. Thus the remnant concept embraces both the Old Testament and New Testament people of faith.

Because of the greater fluidity of the schematic, those embracing salvation-history have a wide range of eschatological options. In general, they affirm inaugurated eschatology: the reign of God began in the person and work of Jesus Christ at his first advent though it will not be consummated until his second advent. Within this general stance premillennialism, amillennialism, and postmillennialism are all possible. Because prophetic literature (not to mention apocalyptic literature) is by its very nature cryptic, dogmatism regarding an eschatological scheme is rare. It is sufficient for salvation-history evangelicals to affirm that Christ's second advent will be personal, visible, and literal, and that all the people of Christian faith will share in resurrection, transformation, and eternal life with God.

The heart of salvation-history's biblical approach is exegesis. Exegesis is controlled by linguistics, archaeology, history, culture, genre, form, sources, redaction, structure, and textual history. For evangelicals the exegetical discipline remains under the authority of Holy Scripture and within the framework of biblical infallibility. They also recognize that exegesis alone does not produce faith. Faith arises as a work of the Holy Spirit. Exegesis can determine the content and theological meaning of

Scripture; only the Holy Spirit can convince a person that such content and theological meaning are the truth.

The Basic Questions

The Kingdom of God

Since most evangelicals fall, more or less, under one of the three systems just described, a brief survey as to how each system answers the basic eschatological questions that tend to divide conservative Christians is in order. The first of these questions is about the kingdom of God. The issue here is whether the kingdom of God is present, future, or in some sense both. Those espousing covenant theology and salvation-history generally see the kingdom of God as already inaugurated in the world during the life and ministry of Jesus. Thus God's rule is now present and active in the world, though it will not reach its consummation until the second advent. Whether premillennial, amillennial, or postmillennial, those who adhere to covenant theology and salvation-history agree that the kingdom must be both present and future in some sense.

Dispensationalists have traditionally seen the kingdom of God as having been genuinely offered to ethnic Israel at Christ's first advent, but withdrawn and postponed until the end of the age because of Israel's rejection of it.[5] The church was born out of Israel's rejection of the kingdom. According to the divine design, the kingdom of God once more will be proclaimed by Jewish evangelists during the great tribulation (after the church is gone from the earth), and the kingdom will be instituted at the second advent (the second phase of Christ's second coming). All the land promises of the Old Testament and their associated blessings will be fulfilled literally in the millennium. The kingdom of God and the millennium thus have a highly Jewish flavor. And teachings about the kingdom, such as the Sermon on the Mount, are sometimes viewed as relating to the kingdom age in the future rather than the ethical behavior of the church in the present.

The Tribulation

The second basic eschatological question has to do with the length and nature of the tribulation, the time of affliction at the close of the age. According to the dispensational interpretation, the entire church age lies in a gap between the end of the sixty-ninth week and the beginning of Daniel's seventieth week, and the tribulation will be exactly seven

years in length. On the other hand, in the nondispensationalist interpretation of the seventy weeks of Daniel as uninterrupted and already
fulfilled in history, the future affliction is of an undetermined length,
though it is often thought to be short.

For the dispensationalist, the tribulation has a highly Jewish character, since it is the time when God turns back to his first people, ethnic
Israel. The church will be with Christ in heaven. A new Jewish temple
will be built on Mount Zion in Jerusalem, Old Testament sacrificial worship under a Jewish priesthood will be revived, and 144,000 Jews will
evangelize the world. Here the beginning of the great tribulation has a
precise starting point, the rapture of the church.

For the nondispensationalist, the time of affliction may be broad
enough to include the destruction of Jerusalem in A.D. 70 and the Roman
imperial persecutions under Domitian and others. Or it may be restricted
to the apocalyptic woes of the Messiah at the end of the age. For those
espousing covenant theology or salvation-history, the tribulation will not
have a Jewish character nor can a precise starting point be specified. It
will simply be a time when the forces of evil collectively assault the people of God. The church will persevere as it awaits the blessed hope of
the second advent.

The Rapture

Another basic question concerns the timing of the rapture of the
church in relationship to the great tribulation. Does the rapture occur
before, in the middle of, or at the end of the period of affliction? For
dispensationalists a pretribulation rapture is a theological necessity to
preserve the separate identities of the two peoples of God, Israel and
the church. The dispensationalist divides the second coming of Christ
into two phases, the coming of Christ for his saints (the rapture) and the
coming of Christ with his saints some seven years later (the return in
glory). The reason why this pretribulational position arose relatively late
in the history of Christian thought is that no biblical passage directly
addresses the relationship between the rapture of the church and the
tribulation.

Midtribulationism begins from the starting point of dispensationalism by accepting the dispensational scheme for Daniel's seventy weeks.
Taking the term "elect" in the Olivet Discourse to be the church,
midtribulationism holds that the church will pass through the first part
of the time of affliction. Generally, this view maintains a careful distinction between tribulation and wrath. The church will experience the great
tribulation (the first half of Daniel's seventieth week), but not the wrath

of God (the last half of Daniel's seventieth week). For midway through the Book of Revelation the church is raptured at the sounding of the seventh trumpet (11:15–19).

Posttribulationism holds that the second coming of Christ will be a single event (as opposed to an event with two stages). The church will endure the time of great affliction at the close of the age. Posttribulationists do not believe, however, that the wrath of God will fall upon the church. Furthermore, while posttribulationists may be premillennial or amillennial, they do not argue for a Jewish character of the millennium. Rather, they see a unity between the people of God in the Old Testament and the people of God in the New Testament.

The Millennium

The basic question with regard to the millennium has to do with the exegesis of a particular passage in Revelation 20:1–6 as well as with the nature and purpose of a utopian age. As is well known from the commentaries, Christians have interpreted the thousand years of Revelation 20:1–6 both literally and symbolically. The nature and purpose of the millennium are even broader theological issues.

For the dispensationalist the millennium is specifically the time when all the promises of land will be fulfilled to ethnic Israel. David (or a son of David or Jesus Christ) will literally reign in Jerusalem over the Jews. Temple worship once more will be conducted with literal blood sacrifices and by a levitical priesthood of legitimate descent. Being premillennial, dispensationalists believe that the millennial reign of Christ cannot begin until his second advent at the end of the age.

The historic premillennialist also looks forward to a literal millennium, but the millennium does not have the Jewish character found in dispensationalism. Rather, it is a time when the triumph of the kingdom of God will be consummated within history following the return of Christ. Human life on earth will take the form for which it was intended in the beginning, a purpose marred by the fall.

The postmillennialist anticipates the conversion of the world to Christianity, a conversion that will usher in a long Christian era. This era, the millennium, will continue until the second coming of Christ at the end of the age. Whereas the dispensationalist and the historic premillennialist are generally pessimistic about the eventual success of Christianity in the world, the postmillennialist is quite optimistic. The former hold that only through the intervention of Christ's second coming is a true millennium possible. The latter holds that a millennium will become a reality through the mission of the Christian church.

The amillennialist interprets the thousand years figuratively. Here the millennium is a symbol of the church age itself, the time when Satan is bound through Christ's victory on the cross. While the duration of the millennium is the same as the church age, its length cannot be calculated precisely.

The Judgments

Finally, there is the basic question about the number of judgments and the groups associated with them. The dispensationalist sees three judgments. First, there is the judgment of the church at the judgment seat of Christ following the rapture, a judgment that will not determine salvation but only the rewards of believers. All who appear at this judgment in heaven will be saved, though their status will vary according to their works. Second, there is the judgment of the nations and Israel at the second advent of Christ in glory. Here the nations will be judged according to their treatment of the Jews during the tribulation period (Matt. 25:31–46). Righteous ethnic Israel will probably be resurrected at this time in order to share in the millennial blessings. Third and last, the wicked will be resurrected and judged after the thousand years.

The historic premillennialist, on the other hand, sees two judgments, the resurrection and reward of God's people at the second advent and the resurrection and damnation of the wicked at the end of the millennium. The righteous of the Old and New Testaments, because they are united in the cross, will stand before the same judgment seat. Finally, amillennialists and postmillennialists see one judgment that will encompass all the living and dead, righteous and unrighteous.

Interpreting Primary Biblical Passages

The foregoing discussion has offered little concerning the interpretation of specific sections of the Bible. It is one thing to describe how different systems answer eschatological questions, but in the end the exegesis of Holy Scripture is decisive. Unable to cover all the relevant passages of Scripture, this work will make some general observations about the basic evangelical systems and their exegetical approaches to five critical eschatological sections of Scripture. These sections are Daniel, the Olivet Discourse, the rapture passages, Revelation, and the millennial passages. It will be sufficient to divide all interpreters into dispensational and nondispensational categories, since the various nondispensational viewpoints have much common ground.

The Book of Daniel

The Book of Daniel with its schematics of history, notably the two visions of the world empires (chs. 2, 7) and the vision of the seventy weeks (ch. 9), has long been recognized as eschatologically important. The book has even been termed "the key to prophetic revelation";[6] while such a conclusion is probably an overstatement, the fact remains that any treatment of eschatology must take into account the remarkable predictions that are found within Daniel. As might be expected, the different systems of prophetic interpretation have varied approaches to its historical schematics.

It should be pointed out from the start that the predictions of Daniel are presented against a backdrop of disillusionment. The book begins with a reference to the exile (Dan. 1:1–2), moves on to describe the fall of Babylon that created the opportunity for the repatriation of the exiles back to Palestine (Dan. 5), and predicts the coming of several great world powers that the Jews would face in the future (Dan. 2, 7, 8, 11). It closes with a vision of the resurrection and exaltation of God's people at the end of history (Dan. 12). All these predictions were delivered to a disillusioned group who had expected the exile to end with a glorious restoration of the Jewish nation to world prominence (cf. Jer. 29:10–14; Isa. 40–55). To be sure, the exiled Jews were allowed to return to their land. Nevertheless, many of the Jews did not return but continued to live in Babylonia and Egypt. Furthermore, for those who did return, times were difficult. Far from becoming the capital of the world, Jerusalem floundered as the pawn of first one political power and then another. The city and its environs were in turn vassals of Persia, Greece, Egypt, Syria, and finally Rome. The prophecies in the Book of Daniel sought to prepare the Jewish people for this bleak future.

In two separate but parallel visions Daniel surveyed the future of world politics. The first vision, actually a dream sent by God to Nebuchadnezzar, depicted the future world empires as metal layers in a huge statue (Dan. 2). The second vision, a dream of Daniel's, depicted the same future world empires as ravenous beasts (Dan. 7):

Daniel 2	Daniel 7
Gold	Lion
Silver	Bear
Bronze	Leopard
Iron	Terrible Beast

These visions have provided considerable grist for the mills of the interpreters. The traditional opinion in the Christian church, dating back to at least Jerome (ca. 347–420), has been generally uniform with respect to these four empires. Babylon was the first, and Medo-Persia the second. Alexander the Great's empire, the Grecian, was the third, while Rome was the fourth. To be sure, in more modern times the suggestion has been offered that the schematic should culminate with the Seleucids of the fragmented empire of Alexander (third and second centuries B.C.), but this viewpoint has not won the support of many evangelicals, since it is based largely on the critical theory that the Book of Daniel was written by someone other than Daniel in the second century rather than the sixth. For most conservatives, it is the detail associated with the fourth empire that has been most controversial. There are two critical interpretive questions at this point. First, is there a fifth empire? And second, what is the nature of the kingdom of God that overcomes all of the previous world empires?

The first question arises because of the detail given about the feet and toes in the first vision and the ten horns in the second vision. While Daniel describes only four empires (2:40; 7:23), dispensationalists usually understand that a fifth empire is implied—the last great empire of world history, an empire to be ruled by the Antichrist after the gap of the church age. The toes of the statue and the horns of the fourth beast are thought to represent this fifth world empire. A current popular interpretation is that this fifth empire is even now being formed in the European Union. Most nondispensationalists do not assume that there is a fifth empire. Rather, they believe that the details associated with the fourth kingdom, Rome, have been historically fulfilled. The ten kings (ten horns) are the Caesars from the time of Julius to Vespasian, and the little horn who is said to oppress the saints is Titus, who destroyed Jerusalem in A.D. 70.

The second question, "What is the nature of the kingdom of God?" is closely related to the first one. In both of Daniel's schematics the climax is the establishment of the kingdom of God in the world. In the first vision, God's kingdom is viewed as a stone that crushes all earthly powers. In the second vision, God's kingdom is established by the Son of man, who descends from heaven, destroys the fourth world empire, and hands the authority of all world powers over to God's people. In keeping with their argument for a fifth world empire at the close of history, dispensationalists interpret the descent of the Son of man as the second coming of Jesus and the beginning of his millennial reign. At his second coming Christ will destroy the empire of the Antichrist and turn over all political power to his people, who will rule and reign with him a thousand years. Nondispensationalists, on the other hand, believe that the kingdom of God was inaugurated during the ministry of Jesus, since Jesus directly identified himself with the figure of the Son of man. In their view, the kingdom of God will destroy all worldly powers when Christ comes the second time. However, the power of the kingdom of God is not reserved exclusively for a future unknown time. It is already active in the world through God's people. Still, though God's kingdom has already been inaugurated, it will not reach its consummation until Christ returns.

Another schematic given by Daniel begins with a decree that the exiled Jews could return to their homeland and rebuild their city (Dan. 9:24–27). It is generally agreed that this schematic, which in the Hebrew text is cryptically described as "seventy sevens," refers to a period of 490 years, that is, 70 periods of 7 years each. This 490-year span is divided into three parts, the first being 49 years long, during which Jerusalem would be restored, the second being an additional 434 years, after which the Messiah would be "cut off," and a final 7 years, during which temple sacrifice would come to a halt. Evangelical scholars generally agree up to this point. Here their agreement ends, however. Some of them view Daniel's figures as symbolic or as round numbers. Thus they escape the difficulty of trying to create precise historical harmonization. Others try to keep intact the idea that the numbers should be harmonized with known history, but in doing so they diverge considerably in making their applications.

According to the dispensational approach, the first 49 years begins with the third decree to restore Jerusalem (Neh. 1:3; 2:3–8). This decree was issued by Artaxerxes in 445 B.C.[7] The 434 years constitutes the period from the rebuilding of Jerusalem until the beginning of Messiah's ministry in about A.D. 26. Next there follows a great gap of undetermined length. This gap, which includes the crucifixion of Jesus and Titus's destruction of Jerusalem in A.D. 70, is referred to as "the great parenthesis." Finally, the last 7 years is the period of the great tribulation at the end of human history. This period is divided into two halves of 3 1/2 years each. At the beginning of this final week, the Antichrist will covenant with the Jews that they may reinstate temple worship. After the first half of the week, however, he will break his agreement with them and turn against them. He will take over the newly constructed Jewish temple and enthrone himself within it as a demigod to be worshiped by the world.

The nondispensational approach to the 490 years is quite different, especially with regard to the final week. The first 49 years is the period from the decree to restore Jerusalem (either the second or third decree) until the completion of Jerusalem's restoration. The 434 years extends from the rebuilding of Jerusalem until the time of the Messiah (late 20s A.D.). The final 7 years, however, begins with Messiah's public ministry and extends only through the early Jewish period of the Christian church. Here there is no great parenthesis; the seventy weeks are continuous. In the middle of the final week the Messiah was cut off (crucified), and because of his once-for-all atonement the Old Testament sacrificial system ended. Sometime after the seventy weeks had ended, Titus destroyed Jerusalem.

It is apparent that there are several critical points of disagreement between these two interpretations. Dispensationalists break the 490 years with a huge gap of at least two millennia between the sixty-ninth and seventieth week. And while the pronoun "he" in 9:27 has no clear antecedent, dispensationalists are certain it refers to the Antichrist. The cessation of sacrifice and oblation is interpreted to mean that the Antichrist will no longer allow Jewish worship in the newly rebuilt temple. Two crucial events occur in the gap between the sixty-ninth and sev-

Figure 3.1
Two Popular Interpretations of the Seventy Weeks

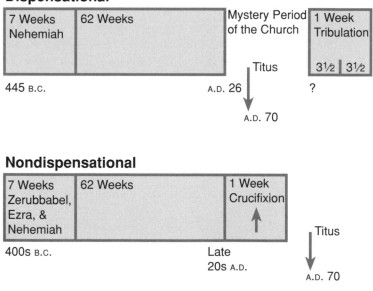

Dispensational

7 Weeks Nehemiah	62 Weeks	Mystery Period of the Church	1 Week Tribulation

445 B.C.   A.D. 26 → Titus   3½ | 3½

A.D. 70   ?

Nondispensational

7 Weeks Zerubbabel, Ezra, & Nehemiah	62 Weeks	1 Week Crucifixion

400s B.C.   Late 20s A.D.   ↑   Titus

A.D. 70

entieth week, the crucifixion of the Messiah and the destruction of Jerusalem by Titus. The seventieth week, which lies in the future, will take the form of 7 years of tribulation at the close of history.

Nondispensationalists do not break up the seventy weeks with hidden gaps. For them, the cessation of sacrifice and oblation is a statement of spiritual truth about the finality of Christ's atonement, which in the eyes of God brought to a close the period of Jewish temple worship. The eventual destruction of the temple by Titus in A.D. 70 was only a historical conclusion to what had already occurred in the spiritual realm. The crucifixion of the Messiah having taken place after 69 1/2 weeks, the final 3 1/2 days were completed in the Jewish period of the early church, which extended into the Christian Era before the first Christians began to break ethnic and nationalistic barriers. As to a tribulation period at the end of history, nondispensationalists address this subject outside the schematic of the seventy weeks.

The Olivet Discourse

The Synoptic Gospels record a discourse Jesus gave while sitting with his disciples on the Mount of Olives during his last days in Jerusalem (Matt. 24:3; Mark 13:3). From this vantage point they could look over the Kidron Valley into the precincts of Herod's temple, and as they sat, Jesus predicted the coming demolition of the temple stone by stone (Matt. 24:2; Mark 13:2; Luke 21:6). The disciples asked when this destruction would occur. From the way in which they framed the question in Matthew's account it is apparent that they assumed the temple would not be destroyed until the end of the age (Matt. 24:3). In the sermon that followed, which is known as the Olivet Discourse, Jesus corrected this mistaken assumption. As we now know, the temple was destroyed not at the end of the age, but by the Roman general Titus in A.D. 70.

While the three Synoptic accounts have much in common, it also should be noted that they are not identical. Both Matthew and Luke give details that are not found in Mark. Also, both Matthew and Luke have unique material. Whereas elsewhere in the Synoptic Gospels the kingdom of God is generally described as being hidden in the present age, all three versions of the Olivet Discourse stress the cosmic events of the last days leading up to the revelation and triumph of the kingdom of God at the close of history. The sermon is apocalyptic in character, drawing directly from the Book of Daniel as well as other Old Testament prophetic material.

In Mark's version it is unclear whether Jesus directly answers the disciples' question about the destruction of Jerusalem. His description of what he calls "the end" is taken by some to refer to the end of Jerusalem and by others to refer to the end of the world (Mark 13:5–23). In favor of the former is the fact that he mentions indictments of his followers by local councils and synagogues, a situation that is particularly relevant to the first century (Mark 13:9). The prediction that some of the disciples would give their witness before magistrates and kings also lends itself easily to a first-century context. The "abomination of desolation," a desecration of the temple described by Daniel (Dan. 9:27; 11:31; 12:11), fits well into the events surrounding Titus's siege of Jerusalem. Against this, however, is the problem that the affliction of the period is described as the worst in the history of the world; it is difficult to believe that, however horrible Titus's siege may have been, it was worse than the holocaust in World War II. On the other hand, those who take Mark's description of the end as referring to the woes at the end of the world have the difficulty of fitting into their scheme such things as the persecution of Christians by local synagogues. Furthermore, they must postulate the construction of yet another Jewish temple, something that neither Jesus nor any one else in the Bible clearly predicted.

Jesus climaxes his discourse in Mark with a description of his return at the close of the age (Mark 13:26–27). William Hendriksen, along with a considerable number of other scholars like R. T. France and D. A. Carson, concludes that in Mark's presentation the siege of Titus and the woes at the end of the age have been conflated into a single account.[8] These two events seem to be inextricably woven together in the sermon, a conflation probably made because the near historical event so appropriately foreshadowed the eschatological one.[9] Others, however, believe that large portions of the discourse are directed to the siege in A.D. 70 and no further. Still others, notably the dispensationalists, take almost everything to refer to the end of the age.

In Mark's version it is also clear that Jesus intended to suppress apocalyptic speculation. This restraint is to be seen in the parenetic phrases of Mark 13:5, 7, 8, 9, 11, 13, 21, 23, 33, 35, and 37. Though the discourse certainly describes a number of future events as precursors to the end of history, the primary purpose of the discourse is not to be a calendar by which one plots the end, but, rather, a strong warning against misunderstanding intermediate events as though they were final ones. Jesus urges his followers to persevere during bad times. He warns against deceptive and false religion (Mark 13:5–6, 21–22), undue alarm because of world catastrophes (Mark 13:7–8, 19–20), and the surrender of faith in the face of persecution (Mark 13:9–13).

In Luke's version, as in Mark's, the near historical event and the distant eschatological event are both in view; however, in Luke there is a clearer focus on the near event. In fact, Luke 21:20–24 is taken by all interpreters to refer to the siege of Jerusalem by Titus in A.D. 70. As in Mark's version Jesus warns against speculation and the attempts to predict the end of the world on the basis of traumatic events that occur during the course of the present age (Luke 21:8–11). Luke's comments about persecution, as in Mark, seem most appropriate for a first-century context (Luke 21:12–19). However, also as in Mark, Luke brings the sermon to a climax with a description of the return of Christ at the very end (Luke 21:25–28). The language regarding the second advent is drawn directly from Daniel's vision of the future world empires (Dan. 7:13–14).

While Luke's version of the discourse stresses the siege by Titus, Matthew's version stresses the second coming of Christ at the end of the age and includes lengthy material unique to the first Gospel (ch. 25). As in the other Synoptics there are warnings against speculation (Matt. 24:4–8). However, while Mark and Luke address the persecution of Christians by local councils and synagogues, Matthew predicts the persecution of Christians by the nations of the world (Matt. 24:9). In Mark's version it is unclear whether the abomination of desolation refers to the near historical event or to the far eschatological one; Matthew's version contains this same ambiguity (Matt. 24:15–25). And also like Mark, Matthew climaxes the discourse with the return of Christ at the end of the age (Matt. 24:26–31).

There remain several interpretive problems unique to the Olivet Discourse that have never been resolved among Christians. One is the specific reference to the abomination originally predicted by Daniel. Does this sacrilege refer to the siege by Titus or to some action of the Antichrist near the end of the age? Also, there is the problem of identifying the persecutions instigated by the synagogues and local councils. Do these persecutions refer to what we already know of early Christian history, as recorded in Acts, or might they allude to something yet future?

Another problem concerns the references to the temple. Jesus repeats Daniel's prediction of a desolating sacrilege to the temple. But what is this temple? Is it Herod's temple that was destroyed by Titus in A.D. 70? (This position seems to have the least difficulties.) Is there yet another Jewish temple, one still to be built in the Holy Land? (This is the conclusion of dispensationalists.) Could the reference be a symbolic allusion to the church, which is the temple of God in a figurative sense? (This conclusion is based upon Paul's metaphor of the church as the temple of God.) How do these references to the temple correlate with Paul's prediction that the man of sin will set himself up in God's temple (2 Thess. 2:4)? All of these questions have been posed and examined by serious Christian interpreters.

Another problem concerns Christ's second coming at the end of the age. Both Matthew and Mark specifically say that it will be after the time of distress (Matt. 24:29–30; Mark 13:24–26). Jesus will come upon the clouds of heaven with great power and glory accompanied by angels who shall gather together his elect from the heavens and the earth (Mark 13:26–27; Matt. 24:30–31; Luke 21:27–28). Does this description also include what is commonly called the rapture of the church (1 Cor. 15:51–55; 1 Thess. 4:15–17; 2 Thess. 2:1)? If so, and this is the kingpin of posttribulationism, then the rapture cannot occur until the tribulation is over.[10] The Olivet Discourse makes no mention of a coming of Christ prior to his return at the end of the age, and certainly gives no hint of his coming prior to the tribulation. Rather, the discourse envisions a single coming of Christ when all of his elect will be gathered to himself. Dispensationalists counter either that the "elect" of God in the discourse refers only to the Jewish people, or that the gathering of God's elect will include the church (from heaven) and the Jews (from the earth). The fact remains, however, that Jesus does not envision a rapture of the church separated from his coming at the end of the age.

Then there is the question about the persecuted people of God. Who are they? Obviously, Jesus spoke directly to the Twelve when he predicted persecution, but was he speaking to them as the future leaders of the Christian church or as believers within the Jewish community? Dispensationalists tend to say that the disciples were being addressed as Jews because the subject at hand was the Jewish temple and the Jewish system. So then, they conclude, the term "the elect" must refer to Jews during the great tribulation. Nondispensationalists, on the other hand, remain firmly convinced that Christians at large are in view throughout the whole discourse. Jesus addresses his disciples as the twelve apostles, that is to say, representatives of his church.

Many take the analogy of the fig tree as referring to climactic events just prior to the end (Mark 13:28–29; Matt. 24:32–33; Luke 21:29–31). Dispensationalists sometimes interpret it as a symbol of the twentieth-century revival of the nation Israel. Indeed, it is not unusual for them to identify the emergence of the State of Israel in 1948 as the "blossoming of the fig tree." However, such an interpretation is oblique at best (see pp. 85–86). Furthermore, in Luke's version Jesus refers to "the fig tree and all the trees," a phrase that is hard to apply specifically to the nation of Israel.

In Matthew, Jesus compares the last days to the time of Noah: life was being carried on normally when the judgment of God was abruptly meted out. It will be the same at the end of the age; "one will be taken and the other left." Yet who will be "taken," and who will be "left"? One interpretation says that the passage describes the rapture of the church—the saints will be taken up into the heavens while the wicked will be left to suffer God's wrath. Another interpretation says that the notion of being "taken" refers to being taken in the judgment of God, just as the wicked in Noah's day were "taken" by the flood (Matt. 24:39). In this view, the one "left" represents the righteous who remain to enjoy the millennial reign of Christ.

What about Jesus' statement that "this generation will certainly not pass away until all these things have happened" (Mark 13:30; Matt. 24:34; Luke 21:32)? If "these things" include the coming of Christ at the end, then how does one define "this generation"? Bypassing Albert Schweitzer and the liberal viewpoint that Jesus was badly mistaken, there are still several possibilities. Dispensationalists once eagerly construed "this generation" to be the generation that would see the sign of the fig tree, which they interpreted as the emergence of Israel as a nation. They fixed the length of a generation as anywhere from twenty-five to forty years. Now that fifty years have passed since 1948, however, this interpretation is increasingly untenable. Others say that "this generation" refers to the Jewish race or, even more generally, to the human race. Probably the most reasonable interpretation is that Jesus was referring to the final generation of history. If so, his statement should be taken to mean that the end will come quickly and not be drawn out. All the final signs and events will be completed within a single generation.

Matthew alone contains the parable of the sheep and goats. Dispensationalists usually see this parable as describing God's judgment of the nations after the tribulation period. They assert that the church will not be involved at all, since it will have previously been raptured and judged. Nondispensationalists usually understand the judgment in Matthew's parable to involve all peoples, including Christians.

The Rapture Passages

In addition to the Olivet Discourse, several passages in the New Testament describe the gathering of Christians to be with Christ at his second coming: 1 Corinthians 15:35–57; 2 Corinthians 5:1–10; 1 Thessalonians 4:13–5:11; and 2 Thessalonians 2:1–12. All four of these passages clearly describe the union of believers with Christ at the end. "At the last trumpet . . . the dead will be raised" (1 Cor. 15:52). This event which "is to come" is associated with the "judgment seat of Christ" (2 Cor. 5:5, 10). "The Lord himself will come down from heaven" (1 Thess. 4:16), and his people with be "gathered to him" (2 Thess. 2:1).

Do these passages provide an answer to the rapture question? The immediate problem is that only one passage (1 Thess.) actually describes the event popularly called "the rapture" of the church. Since pretribulationism is the newest of the interpretations in Christian history, the burden of proof naturally falls on pretribulationists to substantiate their claims. They emphasize the importance of literal interpretation to resolve this issue, but they are hard-pressed to apply it in any decisive way to the actual biblical passages under discussion.[11] The strongest exegetical point in their favor is probably Paul's statement that if the believer's "earthly tent" is destroyed, there is "an eternal house in heaven, not built by human hands" (2 Cor. 5:1). While this may mean no more than that the future destiny of Christians is heaven, it might be taken to mean that at the second coming of Christ believers will meet him in the air and return with him to heaven, which is precisely the dispensational scenario. A second exegetical point raised by pretribulationists concerns the restraining force which is to be removed before the disclosure of the man of lawlessness (2 Thess. 2:6–7). If this restraining force is the church (or the Holy Spirit resident in the church), as pretribulationists usually assert, then the church must be raptured before the tribulation. Unfortunately, there is no direct explanation of the restraining force in the passage, and it has been interpreted variously to refer to the church, the Holy Spirit, civil government, and the binding of Satan. In the end, the plain fact is that Paul is referring to something he had taught when visiting Thessalonica (2 Thess. 2:5). While his readers knew what he was talking about, we do not.

The Thessalonian passages, however, entail significant exegetical difficulties for the pretribulational view. First, Paul uses the word *apantēsis* ("the act of meeting someone") to describe the event (1 Thess. 4:17). This word is a technical term for the ancient civic custom of publicly welcoming important visitors to one's city.[12] What this word envisions is Christians leaving the "gates of the world" to welcome Christ back as he returns to earth. The general usage of this word favors the idea that at the *apantēsis* Christ is welcomed by his church to the earth, just as ambassadors in ancient times would have been welcomed by local dignitaries into the gates of their city.

A second exegetical difficulty is that Paul directly connects "the coming of our Lord Jesus Christ and our being gathered to him" with the "day of the Lord" (2 Thess. 2:1–2). His argument to the Thessalonians seems to be that they should not succumb to hysteria that the day of the Lord has already come. Rather, there are certain preliminary events that must occur first, notably the great apostasy and the disclosure of the man of lawlessness (2 Thess. 2:3–4). Paul seems to assume that some of the Thessalonians might still be alive to see these preliminary events—events which all agree will occur within the tribulation period.

A third exegetical difficulty is that Paul seems to use the words denoting the second coming (*parousia, epiphany,* and *apocalypse*) interchangeably in a way that discourages the theory that there are two phases. Dispensationalists tend to use *parousia* to refer to the rapture prior to the tribulation and *epiphany* and *apocalypse* to refer to Christ's appearance at the end of the tribulation. Paul, on the other hand, speaks of the *"epiphany of Christ's parousia"* (2 Thess. 2:8). In several corollary passages he clearly indicates that the hope of the church is not only the *parousia* of Christ, but also his *epiphany* (1 Tim. 6:14; 2 Tim. 4:8; Titus 2:13) and *apocalypse* (1 Cor. 1:7; 2 Thess. 1:6–7; see also 1 Peter 1:7, 13; 4:13).

Figure 3.2
Two Views of the Rapture and Christ's Return

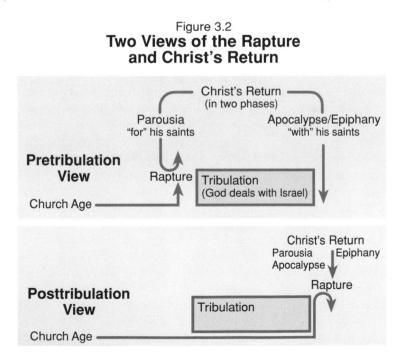

Whatever decision the interpreter makes regarding the rapture question, one thing is clear. It is very hard to produce an argument compelling enough to win consensus when there is only a single passage which describes the event. In general, one's opinion about the rapture is formed on grounds other than exegetical. It is formed by appealing to one or another of the basic systems of eschatological thought.

The Book of Revelation

Doubtless the most famous of all prophetic books is the Apocalypse of John. The document is written in the style of Jewish apocalyptic, and like other such literature abounds with esoteric and cryptic disclosures about the end of the world. Apocalyptic works seek to depict the ultimate triumph of God's people over the powers of evil, climaxing with the establishment of God's kingdom on earth at the end of the age. The Book of Revelation is no exception. It is replete with symbolism, particularly animal symbolism and numerology. It describes cosmic disturbances and allows the reader to look behind the veil of the spirit world to view the activities of angels and demons. In particular, it describes the conflict between the powers of evil, which dominate this present age, and the purposes of God, which will be accomplished in the age to come.

The primary question, of course, is one of interpretation. Given the cryptic and esoteric nature of the literature, the reader faces a formidable task in trying to discern the message of the book for its first readers, which is the primary goal of all interpretation. Of course, if we knew for certain how the earliest Christians read the book, we would be a long way toward establishing a valid meaning for the church today. Unfortunately, all that we know for sure is that the postapostolic church expected that the Christian community would see the whole complex of events described in the book, including the rise of the Antichrist, the tribulation, and the return of Jesus to judge the world. They understood the book to predict the end of the world and the suffering of the church at the hands of Antichrist beforehand.[13]

Although the specific details of the Revelation may bear many potential meanings, there are in general five basic approaches to the book. The first is idealism, which construes the symbolism of Revelation in the most general of terms and largely separates it from any particular historical situation. Idealism sees the book as describing the spiritual conflict between God's people and the powers of evil. The satanic activities in the book do not refer to any particular outbreak against the church as much as they typify every such outbreak in a timeless way. For the book is concerned with ideas and principles, not with specific events and historical figures. It is poetic in the most abstract sense of the word. A form of idealism dominated the medieval period of the church when the allegorical method of interpretation was in vogue. Since that time the idealist approach has had greater and lesser degrees of popularity; at present it is less popular than the others.[14]

The greatest advantage of idealism is at the same time its greatest liability. Though the denial that there is any specific historical content in Revelation saves the interpreter from quibbling over details, it prevents the interpreter from treating seriously the apocalyptic character of the book. While being especially concerned with events that lead to the end of the age, Jewish apocalyptic seeks to identify such events in contemporary history that threaten to overwhelm God's people. One would expect the Book of Revelation to do the same.

Historicism, a second approach, is the view that the symbols of Revelation refer to major events in the history of Christian Europe. The historicist generally sees the book as addressing the interval between Christ's first and second comings. The beast of chapter 13, for instance, has at different times been identified with Muhammad, Luther, Napoleon, and Hitler. During the Protestant Reformation the historicist view became increasingly tied to the antipapal struggles of the Reformers. The beast was interpreted to be the papacy, and the false prophet was the Roman Catholic Church. This view became so widely held by Protestants that for a long time it was dubbed "the Protestant view." Protestant historicists held that the Revelation describes the struggle between true and false religion in the Western world.[15]

Historicism's greatest weakness is that it ends up being largely irrelevant to its first readers, or for that matter to anyone outside Europe. It is difficult to understand why a group of churches in Asia Minor should be informed of events a thousand years away and in another part of the globe. Second, this approach almost completely ignores the character of apocalypticism, preferring to devise its own interpretations without reference to the normative elements of apocalyptic literature. Finally, it suffers from subjectivism: its proponents have major disagreements about historical fulfilments.

Preterism, a third approach, is the prevailing interpretation of modern critical scholars.[16] They see the Revelation as addressing the situation of the early churches and especially the overwhelming opposition they faced from imperial Rome. The beast was one of the Roman emperors, and the false prophet was the cult of emperor worship. Revelation, like other apocalyptic writings, was a tract for bad times. It was written for a concrete historical situation at the end of the first century, not as a prediction of far-flung history. It assured the church that her present tribulation would be short and that God was in control. The Lord would soon intervene to vindicate his people.

The major weakness of the preterist view is that it does not take seriously that Revelation is both apocalyptic and prophetic. While recognizing the relevance of the book's apocalypticism to the historical situation of its first readers, preterism largely ignores the prophetic element or devalues it as speculation that failed to materialize.

Whereas allegorical interpretation dominated the medieval period and historicism dominated the Reformation and post-Reformation periods, futurism came to dominate Protestantism in the nineteenth century. It is still the most popular approach in many conservative churches. A particular kind of futurism, dispensationalism, views the Book of Revelation as largely concerned with what will happen on the earth after the rapture has occurred. True, some dispensationalists tend to view the letters to the seven churches as symbols of seven eras of church history (see pp. 74–76). The bulk of the book, however, describes the struggle between the Jews and the Antichrist during the projected seven-year tribulation that corresponds to the seventieth week of Daniel.[17]

The major weakness of dispensationalism is that while it takes seriously the prophetic character of the book, it does not do justice to its apocalyptic character. If the Revelation is primarily about the struggle between the Jews and the Antichrist in a century far removed from the early church, it is hard to see why the book would have been written to seven local congregations in Asia Minor. Further, the dispensationalist tendency to interpret passages from the Revelation quite specifically in terms of twentieth-century political events or trends is prone to subjectivism and the manipulation of Scripture to fit a particular theory. Many such interpretations associated with the Cold War of the 1950s–1980s already have proved false.

Historic premillennialism, a fifth approach, attempts to hold together both the prophetic and the apocalyptic character of Revelation, thus making it relevant to the first congregations who read it as well as to the church at large that awaits Christ's return. This approach seeks to go back to the general position of the postapostolic church. Like dispensationalism, historic premillennialism is premillennial, but unlike dispensationalism, it is posttribulational. It views Revelation as an extended double entendre, that is, as describing the struggle between the early church and imperial Rome, yet at the same time as foreshadowing the struggle between the church and the powers of evil at the end of the age.

It agrees with the futuristic perspective that the book primarily describes the consummation of God's redemptive purpose.[18]

In spite of these markedly different approaches, most interpreters of the Revelation agree regarding the basic theology of the book. Like Jesus and Paul (Matt. 24:15–31; 2 Thess. 2:3–12), the book anticipates a brief period of terrible evil, comparable to the struggle of the early church with imperial Rome but on a much grander scale. Society will be overwhelmed by satanically inspired agents who will openly defy God and seek to divert all worship toward Satan, themselves, and the state. Terrible martyrdom awaits those who do not conform. With unrelenting enmity the powers of evil will be unleashed upon the people of God.

However, evil is not the only force at work. God shall unleash upon the world judgments of his own, not unlike those he leveled against Egypt at the time of the exodus. Just as Pharaoh set himself against Yahweh, so the beast and his cohorts shall oppose Christ and his people. But in the end God's people will be delivered when the Lord Jesus Christ comes in glory at his second advent. All the earthly kingdoms and their power will then be passed over to Christ Jesus and his followers, who will rule and reign with him in righteous triumph.

Commentaries on the Book of Revelation are not wanting. From conservatives to liberals, from dispensationalists to amillennialists, from historicists to futurists, theologians and scholars have produced works on this fascinating and perplexing book. A common flaw in these treatments, most of which are exegetical and expositional, is their failure to interact with the various viewpoints for assessing the theological problems that arise in interpreting the book.

Among the most critical exegetical issues handled by the commentaries is when the book was written. The question of dating is more than just a matter of historical fact. The time of writing figures significantly in what one takes the book to mean. For instance, if the book was written in the late 60s A.D. (as some scholars think), then much of the content must be read against the background of Nero's mad persecution of the Christians in Rome. Furthermore, Jerusalem had not yet fallen at that time. If, on the other hand, the book was written in the late 90s A.D. (as the majority of scholars think), then it must be read against the background of the cult of Caesar worship. The first Jewish revolt and the fall of Jerusalem would have been two decades in the past.

Whether the background of Revelation is the 60s or the 90s bears upon several critical passages in the book. There is little doubt that the "seven hills," as a common designation from antiquity, refers to Rome (Rev. 17:9), but who is the sixth potentate who now "is" (Rev. 17:10)?

Is it Nero, Domitian, or someone else? What about the reference to the "temple of God" (Rev. 11:1)? Does it have in view a temple in Jerusalem still standing in the lifetime of the author? Or is it a spiritual metaphor for the church or perhaps a temple to be built sometime in the future? The same kind of question attends the reference to the "holy city" (Rev. 11:2). Does it look to ancient Jerusalem or something else? As one can see, the question of dating directly connects with interpreting the book. Some within the early church believed that the book was written in the late 90s A.D.[19] While this date is not absolutely certain, it has won the majority of scholars.

Also crucial to interpretation are the book's claims to be a letter, a prophecy, and an apocalypse. As a letter the Revelation was addressed to seven particular congregations in Asia Minor: Ephesus, Smyrna, Pergamum, Thyatira, Sardis, Philadelphia, and Laodicea (Rev. 1:4). It was intended to be read aloud in public (Rev. 1:3), just as were other New Testament letters (cf. Col. 4:16). We should assume, then, that the contents of the Revelation had historical significance for its first readers. It could hardly be otherwise. Any group of Christians to whom a letter was addressed and before whom it then was read publicly could hardly fail to apply its contents to themselves. Otherwise, what would be the point?

As a prophecy (Rev. 1:3; 22:7, 10, 18–19) the book also contains predictions about the future. While as a letter it addresses its first readers and their times, as a prophecy it addresses what still lies ahead. This future is described as "what must soon take place," as "near," and as "soon" (Rev. 1:1, 3; 22:6, 10, 20). Since it is directly connected with the second coming of Christ (Rev. 1:7; 2:25; 3:3, 11; 16:15; 22:7, 12, 20), most interpreters take this future to be coming "soon" in the sense that it is always impending. Such a sophisticated reading seems necessary in light of the fact that there have already been two millennia of Christian history, though it is not clear that the first readers had this understanding. It seems more likely that they took the references as pointing to the return of Christ in their own lifetimes (cf. John 21:22–23).

Now to read the book both as a letter and as a prophecy produces a tension. How much of it refers to the original readers' times, and how much refers to the indeterminate future? The best solution seems to be to view the Revelation as referring both to the late-first-century struggle between Christians and imperial Rome and also, by foreshadowing, to the struggle between the people of God and the forces of evil at the end of the age. Interpreters differ as to which of these two eras receives the greater emphasis in Revelation. On the one extreme, the dispensationalist sees very little of the book as relating to the first century and most of it as relating to the end of the age. At the other extreme, the preterist sees most of it as relating to the first century and little of it as foreshadowing the end of history.

The book is also an apocalypse (Rev. 1:1). The apocalypse, as a literary genre, aimed at disclosing the secrets of the hidden world. It was especially intended to offer behind-the-scenes insight into the struggle between God and the powers of evil that raged in human history. It assured God's people that while evil might seem to prevail in the present, the triumph of God was assured in the end. For the time being, however, the faithful must contend with cosmic disturbances and the work of demons.

Following the letters to the seven churches there appears the intriguing expression, "I will show you what must take place after this" (Rev. 4:1b). This statement must surely connect with Isaiah's and Paul's promise that, in the end, every knee will bow and every tongue confess the sovereignty of God—in Pauline terms, every tongue will "confess that Jesus Christ is Lord, to the glory of God the Father" (Isa. 45:22–25; Phil. 2:9–11).

Dispensationalists, with their commitment to a pretribulation rapture, see yet a further significance here. They often view the twenty-four elders (Rev. 4:4, 10–11) as symbolizing the raptured church in heaven just prior to the seven years of tribulation on earth. While the world below is convulsed in distress, the raptured church is enthralled in worship. Thus the events described in the remainder of the book belong to the future entirely. Exegetically, however, there is little to recommend this view. The elders in heaven always seem to be distinguished from "the saints" rather than identical to them (Rev. 5:8; 11:16–18; 19:1–4). The more common view among expositors is that the priestly elders represent a special group of spirit-beings belonging to the general class of angels. Inasmuch as they are positioned between the cherubim and the general host of angels, this interpretation seems compelling.

In chapter 6 we begin to read of the opening of the seven seals, which are precursors to the end. The first four seals are depicted as horsemen. This imagery is taken from the Book of Zechariah, where four horsemen, patterned after the patrols of the Persian Empire, report to the Lord about the conditions upon earth (Zech. 1:7–11). The horsemen in Revelation are not merely reporting patrols, however. They symbolize the trauma of conquest, war, famine, and plague (Rev. 6:2–8). The other seals depict martyrdom (Rev. 6:9–11), cosmic disruption (Rev.

6:12–17), and preparation for seven other terrible judgments (Rev. 8:1–5).

The crucial question, of course, is when these things shall happen. There are three schools of thought. One is that they actually did happen in the destruction of Jerusalem in A.D. 70. Josephus's description of the fall of Jerusalem to the Roman general Titus is coupled with passages in Luke's version of the Olivet Discourse (Luke 21:20–26) to suggest that the entire scope of the seals is locked within the first century. Another viewpoint is that all these woes will occur just prior to the second coming of Christ. The Olivet Discourse describes many of the same cosmic disturbances (Matt. 24:29; Mark 13:24–25; Luke 21:25–26) as preceding Christ's second coming (Matt. 24:30; Mark 13:26; Luke 21:27). For those who view the final chapter of human history as the seventieth week of Daniel, the seals fall within this seven-year period. Yet a third viewpoint is that these woes characterize the general course of the age, though they escalate as the end approaches. This viewpoint merits some further explanation.

The Olivet Discourse may bear directly upon the interpretation of the seven seals with their predictions of catastrophic events and cosmic disturbances. In the discourse Jesus responds to his disciples' question about what "sign" is to be expected before "the end," though interpreters disagree about whether "the end" refers to the end of the age or the coming destruction of Jerusalem. Jesus warns against speculation (Mark 13:5, 7, 8, 9, 11, 13, 21, 23, 33, 35, 37). Certainly there will be precursors. Such precursors always warn the righteous that the time "is near" (Mark 13:29), but this time is not so much a date to be calculated as a future event to be constantly affirmed and watched for (Mark 13:32–37).

Of these three interpretations, the first two attempt to pinpoint the specific time of fulfilment (either A.D. 70 or the period following the rapture of the church). The third one does not attempt to be precise. If true, it means that the opening of the seals has already begun. The escalation of conquests, wars, famines, earthquakes, and martyrdoms characterizes the whole of world history from the time of Jesus until the present. If, as some interpreters think, the cataclysms of the sun, moon, and stars are symbols of social and political disruption, then such disruptions are already in process during the present age. However, one should not be too quick to dismiss the possibility of a literal disruption of the cosmic bodies.

The parallel interludes between the sixth and seventh seal (ch. 7) and between the sixth and seventh trumpet (Rev. 10:1–11:14) heighten the suspense. Both describe the people of God during the tumultuous woes of Messiah. In the interlude of chapter 7, the people of God are depicted in two ways, first as 144,000 servants of God from the twelve tribes who are sealed for protection during the great afflictions before the end (Rev. 7:1–8), and second as the triumphant multitude of the redeemed from among the nations who survive the great tribulation (Rev. 7:9–17). In the first case the people of God are depicted as Israel (Rev. 7:4), in the second as Gentiles (Rev. 7:9). Most interpreters agree that these depictions describe believers who live through the woes associated with the opening of the seals, both because the description is sandwiched between the sixth and seventh seal, and because the latter group is described as having passed through "great tribulation" (Rev. 7:14). Nevertheless, there are two related questions that divide interpreters. First, do the two depictions refer to the same group by different metaphors, or are there in fact two different groups? Second, who, then, are these people of God?

Typical dispensational interpretations hold that the two groups are different, the first being Israelites (because God will return to his Jewish people during the seventieth week of Daniel after the church is raptured), and the second being the non-Jewish multitudes who come to faith because of the Jewish testimony during the seventieth week. Neither group, then, represents the church per se.

Nondispensationalists object that nothing in the passage suggests that the 144,000 are evangelists or that the international multitude are their converts. Furthermore, the figures in this passage are symbolic numbers typical of apocalyptic. The number 144,000 may be directly related to the vision of the Holy City, the Lamb's wife, which is depicted as a cube and measures 12,000 stadia on each of its 12 edges (Rev. 21:16—12,000 x 12 = 144,000). The 144,000 are described as "Israel" because the church is the new Israel, headed by the twelve apostles (cf. Gal. 6:16). They are sealed with the Father's name, the mark of Christians (Rev. 3:12; 14:1). The first description depicts the sealing of Christians for protection during the woes of Messiah; the second description is a preview of their final triumph at the end. They are at once "the Israel of God" and the multitude of Christian believers "from every nation, tribe, people and language."

Again and again the hermeneutical issue of identifying people groups within the visions of John is critical. In chapter 11 there are the two witnesses, obviously patterned after Zerubbabel and Joshua (Zech. 3:1; 4:3–5, 8–9, 12–14; Rev. 11:4) on the one hand, and Moses and Elijah on the other (Exod. 7:20; Deut. 18:15; 1 Kings 17:1; 2 Kings 1:10, 12; Mal. 4:5; Rev. 11:5–6). Interpreters are divided over whether the two witnesses represent individual persons or groups. Those who interpret them as individuals usually believe them to be Moses and Elijah because of the mysterious circumstances of their last moments on earth (Deut. 34:5–6; Jude 9; 2 Kings 2:11), or Enoch and Elijah, the two Old Testament characters who did not die. Or the two witnesses may be two individuals yet to arise who will have the powers of Moses and Elijah.

On the other hand, if the two witnesses refer to groups (or some particular group), the most natural interpretation is that they represent the church, God's new covenant people to whom Moses and Elijah testify (cf. Matt. 17:3; Mark 9:4; Luke 9:30–31). This interpretation leans heavily on the reversal of Jewish-Gentile symbolism both in this passage and in the rest of the Apocalypse. Jerusalem, the capital city of Israel since the time of David, has become an unbelieving pagan community typified as Sodom and Egypt (Rev. 11:8). The temple, with its priesthood and furnishings that were once exclusively reserved for Jewish worship, symbolically has become the Christian church (Rev. 1:6, 20; 3:12; 5:10; 6:9; 7:15). The ark is now in heaven, not on earth (Rev. 11:19). The old sacrifices of Torah have been replaced by a single universal sacrifice, the Lamb slain (Rev. 5:6). In fact, the category of Jewishness itself has been reversed (2:9; 3:9). If this reversal bears upon the temple scene in 11:1, then the worshipers in the temple are Christians who are protected until their Christian witness has been completed (Rev. 11:5a). The two witnesses symbolize the church in its evangelistic testimony. The beast that attacks the witnesses is pagan Rome, which persecuted the early church, and in a double entendre it is also the kingdom of Antichrist that shall rise against the church at the end of the age. At the end the church will be resurrected from the dust of martyrdom, ascending into heaven at the call of God (Rev. 11:12). The earthly city of Jerusalem, which has now become pagan, will collapse (Rev. 11:13).

Yet another debated figure is the pregnant woman clothed with the sun (Rev. 12:1–2). In ancient times the imagery of a pregnant woman facing a dragon was an internationally known symbol depicting the struggle between the righteous and the powers of evil. This imagery is also to be found in the Old Testament, where a pregnant woman struggles to give birth to the messianic people and the messianic age (Isa. 26:17–18; 66:7–13; Mic. 4:10–12).

Who is this woman? Interpretations have ranged from Israel to the Christian church to the Virgin Mary. The clearest indications are to be found in Revelation 12:1, which recalls Joseph's dream in which the sun, moon, and twelve stars represented, respectively, Jacob, Rachel, and the sons of Israel (Gen. 37:9); and in Revelation 12:5, where the male child who was born of the woman and who would rule the nations with an iron scepter is a clear reference to the Messiah from David's line (Ps. 2:7–9). That the woman is the Virgin Mary seems unlikely given the statements in Revelation 12:6, 13–16, where she seems to represent the persecuted people of God who will be protected for three-and-a-half years. The dream of Joseph fits with the interpretation that the woman is Israel, but her persecution following the ascension of Christ does not. The persecution of the woman and her offspring who "hold to the testimony of Jesus" fits the interpretation that she is the persecuted church (12:6, 13–17; 20:4), but it is difficult to see how the church can be said to give birth to the Messiah. Perhaps the best approach is to simply avoid the rigid distinction between Israel and the church and to view the woman as representing the people of God. If so, she represents all of God's people.

At various intervals in the Book of Revelation the reader meets groups of people called "saints." Who are they? Because the term "saint" is somewhat generic, various interpretations are possible. Dispensational-ists are convinced that they are Jews who have turned to Christ during the final period of tribulation. Others, especially in light of descriptions like "saints . . . who bore testimony to Jesus" (Rev. 17:6, 14; 19:10) and "saints and apostles and prophets" (Rev. 18:20, 24), believe they are Christians who live during the time of terrible oppression. The blessing upon those who "die in the Lord from now on" (Rev. 14:13) recalls the martyrs who were killed for their testimony (Rev. 6:9). The various references to the saints, those sealed by God, the martyrs, the triumphant 144,000, and those having the testimony of Jesus are thought to be the same group, Christians who struggle against the powers of evil, whether in ancient Rome at the close of the first century or in the world during the final period of the age. They are the victorious Christian martyrs who have been faithful unto death (Rev. 2:10). They have completed their final exodus over the sea of fiery trial, refusing to surrender to the beast and his mark (Rev. 15:1–2). Just as Moses once led his people across the Red Sea, the Lamb has led his faithful followers to victory through mar-tyrdom (Rev. 15:3–4). The only thing remaining is for those who killed them to be dealt the seven final plagues, symbolized by seven golden bowls of divine wrath that will be poured out upon a wicked world (Rev. 15:5–8).

Finally, near the end of the book comes the millennial vision of the thousand years of Satan's imprisonment and the reign of God's saints. The epilogue stresses that the events of the Book of Revelation are "near" (Rev. 22:6, 7, 10, 12, 20). The end is always at hand. In the meantime

God's people must continue to live in righteousness and holiness as they wait for the consummation (Rev. 22:7, 11, 14). The visions heralding the end are for the churches (Rev. 22:16), and the invitation to follow the Lamb is to anyone who wills (Rev. 22:17).

The Millennial Passages

No issue is more tied to the particular eschatological systems than is the millennial issue. In the strictest sense possible, there is only a single passage that describes the thousand years (Rev. 20:1–10). Yet there are dozens of passages in both the Old and New Testaments that, depending upon the system held by the interpreter, may refer to the period indirectly. One's conclusion about the millennial question depends in turn upon conclusions about the nature of the kingdom of God and the purpose of God in history. So the question is far more than merely an exegetical one, though it certainly is that as well.

For the postmillennialist the Great Commission of Christ to the church was more than just a formal task (Matt. 28:19). It was also intended to turn hearts to Christ so that the world would become truly Christian. To expect the Christianization of the world is not to say that all sin will be abolished, but it is to anticipate that the powers of evil will be reduced to negligible proportions by the work of the Holy Spirit through the church. Though not everyone will become a believer, the dominant worldview will be Christian. Because the prophets said that the nations would be joined together in the common worship of the one true God, this will happen within history through the testimony of the Christian church (Ps. 2:8; 22:27–31; Isa. 2:2–4; 11:6–9; Mic. 4:2–5; Zech. 9:9–10; 14:9–21). Jesus' statement that the gates of hell will not prevail against the church means that the church will conquer the world (Matt. 16:18). And his great prayer for God's will to be done on earth as in heaven will be fulfilled through his church (Matt. 6:10). This golden age will not come suddenly, but gradually, through the mission of the church. Passages that lend themselves to this interpretation include Romans 11:25–26, where Paul envisions a mass conversion of Jews to Christianity, and Romans 5:12–19, where Paul argues that just as Adam's fall brought death to all, so Jesus' obedience brings life to all. Of the various millennial views, postmillennialism is without question the most optimistic.

The amillennialist and the postmillennialist have much in common. Both tend to interpret key elements in Revelation 20:1–10 in approximately the same way. They argue that since so many other numbers in the book are symbolic, this period should be interpreted symbolically too. The binding of Satan with the great chain and the reign of Christ's saints depict conditions during the age of the church. The thousand years symbolizes the church age, a period when Satan has been defeated through the work of Christ on the cross (John 12:31; 14:30; 16:11). Rather than 365 days each, the thousand years will simply be a very long time, the time of the church in the world until the return of Christ, a time when believers already "have become kings" (1 Cor. 4:8). At the very end of the church age, Satan once again will be allowed to attack the people of God (Rev. 20:7–9), and this final conflict is what the Book of Revelation is about. The final event following the church age will be the great judgment (Rev. 20:11–15). Accepting this interpretation, amillennialists do not look forward to a thousand-year period in the future. In their viewpoint it is already in process, and hence some would prefer the term "realized millennialism" as a more accurate description. Amillennialists are not as optimistic as postmillennialists, however. Whereas postmillennialists look for the conversion of most people in the world to Christianity, amillennialists affirm a continuing tension between Christ and his enemies until the second coming.

Premillennialists believe that the thousand years will follow the war in Revelation 19; if so, the thousand years are still future, since there is a general consensus that chapter 19 describes the second coming of Jesus. Dispensational premillennialists tend to interpret the thousand years as normal calendar years. Historic premillennialists, in light of other elements taken as symbols (e.g., the chain binding Satan, the key to the Abyss), tend to interpret the thousand years as a long period of time. Dispensational premillennialists fit all the promises of land to Abraham and his posterity into the millennium; consequently, the millennium has a very Jewish character. Historic premillennialists tend to see these same promises fulfilled in the church; while they may, on the basis of passages like Romans 11:17–32, be open to the idea that God will perform a special work among the Jews, they do not cast the millennium in such stark Jewish character. Both dispensational premillennialists and historic premillennialists agree that the millennium will be the consummation of the kingdom of God within history. Unlike postmillennialists they do not believe that the consummation will come by gradual transition, but by the cataclysmic return of the Lord. Premillennialists, at least when compared to the postmillennial optimism, tend to be pessimistic about the success rate of the Christian church.

Exegetically, much hangs upon the interpretation of the phrases "came to life" and "first resurrection" (Rev. 20:4–6). If they refer to regeneration or, alternatively, to the spiritual reign of martyrs in heaven during the church age, as postmillennialists and amillennialists often take them, then the Book of Revelation does not hold forth a vision for a future millennium. However, if the coming to life and the first resurrection refer to a bodily resurrection which occurs after the war in Revelation 19, then the Book of Revelation does in fact anticipate a millennium after the second coming of Jesus.

Does It Matter?

Vincent of Lérins (died ca. A.D. 450) coined the Latin phrase "quod ubique, quod semper, quod ab omnibus creditum est," which defines the faith of the Christian church as "that which has been believed everywhere, always, by all." Similar definitions appear in other writings of the church fathers. It is apparent, of course, that these early Christian leaders were not referring to all the ideas and theologies that Christians might have. The first several centuries of the Christian church saw quite a number of notions rise and fall that could never fit the description of "that which has been believed at all times and in all places." Still, there was an essential core of primary theological truths that the Fathers believed defined the Christian church. Particularly in the face of heresies and distortions the early Christians came to summarize what they believed. One finds this tendency even in the New Testament in passages such as Acts 8:37; 1 Corinthians 12:3; 15:1–4; and 1 Timothy 3:16. Later Christians became more elaborate in their formulations. Aristides (before A.D. 138), for example, wrote in his defense of Christianity: "They [Christians] trace their origins to the Lord Jesus Christ. He is confessed to be the Son of the most high God, who came down from heaven by the Holy Spirit and was born of a virgin and took flesh, and in a daughter of man there lived the Son of God. . . . This Jesus . . . was pierced by the Jews, and he died and was buried; and they say that after three days he rose and ascended into heaven. . . . They believe God to be the Creator and Maker of all things, in whom are all things and from whom are all things."[20] Outsiders also frequently called for statements of what Christians believed, much as today one will ask for a particular church's statement of faith.

One of the most important outlines which summarized early Christian belief was called the "rule of faith," or alternatively, "the faith," "the tradition," "the preaching," or "the rule of truth." This outline was believed to have been handed down unbroken and unaltered from the apostles. While there were several variations, depending upon which heresy was being combated in what place, the rule of faith was intended to describe the basic essence of Christian belief. More than likely, it was used as a profession of faith at Christian baptisms. In fact, Hippolytus's account of Christian baptism near the beginning of the third century indicates that candidates for baptism were asked questions based on the rule of faith. To the question "Do you believe in God the Father Almighty?" the candidate responded, "I believe," which was followed by the first immersion. The next question was, "Do you believe in Christ Jesus, the Son of God, who was born by the Holy Spirit of the Virgin Mary, and was crucified under Pontius Pilate, and was dead and buried, and rose again the third day, alive from the dead, and ascended into heaven, and sat at the right hand of the Father, and will come to judge the living and the dead?" The candidate responded, "I believe," which was followed by the second immersion. On responding to the final question, "Do you believe in the Holy Spirit, in the holy church, and the resurrection of the body?" the candidate was then immersed again.[21]

Notice the kinds of doctrines that the rule of faith sought to protect. Against the Gnostic notion of creation by an inferior deity, the rule of faith affirmed that the universe was created by God the Father. Against the Ebionites, who rejected the virgin birth and deity of Jesus Christ, it affirmed both to be true. Against the Gnostic doubt of the death of Jesus on the cross and his resurrection from the dead, it affirmed that he truly died and truly arose. Against the sectarians who divided the church, it affirmed the catholicity of the church. Against the Manichaeans, who denied the resurrection of the body, it affirmed the hope of resurrection. Thus the rule of faith largely was shaped as an orthodox response to the distortions of Christian teaching which were developing all around.

The rule of faith was not a creed with fixed wording, but eventually creeds with fixed wording adapted from the baptismal questions and the rule of faith were adopted. The most significant early creed, dating from about the mid-fourth century in its earliest form, is popularly known as the Apostles' Creed. It summarizes the central confessional teachings of the apostles (see Matt. 28:19; Acts 8:37; 16:31; Rom. 10:9; 1 Cor. 8:6; 15:3–4; 2 Cor. 13:14; Eph. 4:4–5; Phil. 2:10–11; 1 Tim. 2:5–6; 3:16; 6:13–14; 2 Tim. 2:8; 1 Peter 3:18; 1 John 5:1). *What is to be especially observed is that none of these confessions, either formal or informal, required a particular eschatological system.* To be sure, they contained phrases affirming the resurrection of the body and the judgment of the living and the dead. Aristides even articulated what Justo Gonzalez has called "a sharp eschatological expectation": in his apology to the Roman emperor Hadrian he anticipated a "terrible judgment which will come upon all mankind through Jesus." He could even assert that the world continued to subsist only on account of the prayers of the Christians.[22] Still, such statements hardly advocate a sophisticated eschatological system with a detailed calendar of the end of the world. Among contemporary Christians there is still ongoing discussion about what elements belong at the core of the Christian faith, but in light of the essential teachings of the postapostolic church, we cannot argue that a particular system of eschatology is one of them.

A brief excursion into the writings of Justin Martyr (d. A.D. 165) illustrates the point admirably. When Trypho the Jew asked whether Justin really believed that ancient Jerusalem would be rebuilt and inhabited by Christ, Christians, the patriarchs, and the prophets for a thousand years, Justin wrote in response, "I and many others are of this opinion and [believe] that such will take place. . . . But, on the other hand, I signified to you that many who belong to the pure and pious faith, and are true Christians, think otherwise."[23] Two millennia later, true Christians still "think otherwise" on all sorts of eschatological issues. *There is consensus among conservative Christians that the personal, literal, and visible second coming of Jesus belongs in the essential core of doctrine, but beyond that the consensus breaks down.*

The various eschatological systems superimposed upon the text of Scripture attempt to provide interpretations of the biblical data that are cohesive, logical, and plausible. Since these systems sharply differ at various points, it is clear that they cannot all be right. In fact, we must recognize the possibility that while they all cannot be right, they all could be wrong. Thus it is critical that Christians not establish any eschatological system at the center of theology. The center of theology is Jesus Christ, God's Son, the Savior of the world. To be sure, part of the Bible's clear teaching about him is that he will come again, but the timing and the surrounding events are ambiguous.

Someone may well ask then, "Is the study of eschatology even appropriate?" Certainly it is. The study of all subjects in the Bible is worthy, but not all are at the center of the church's faith. The wise Christian will perceive the differences between primary and secondary issues, and will realize that many if not most of the eschatological issues that are so hotly debated are secondary. Theological humility is in order, a point expressed most articulately by Adam Clarke long before most of the modern eschatological systems were even on the table. In his commentary on the Revelation, after surveying several of the popular historicist approaches then in vogue, Clarke wrote, "My readers will naturally expect that I should either give a decided preference to some one of the opinions stated above, or produce one of my own; I can do neither, nor can I pretend to explain the book: I do not understand it; and in the things which concern so sublime and awful a subject, I dare not, as my predecessors, indulge in conjectures."[24] Of course, this sentiment did not prevent him from writing his commentary, and from the vantage point of a century and a half later, it seems that he did occasionally "indulge in conjectures." That observation notwithstanding, his expression of open humility is a rare and beautiful thing.

The honest student of the Bible must confess that there are considerable ambiguities in its eschatological sections. One should admit such ambiguities, if for no other reason than that there are such a variety of systems and opinions available. The biblical writers indicate again and again that ambiguity concerning the details of the future is to be expected. Take, for example, the messages in the later chapters of Isaiah. "Who has understood the Spirit of the LORD, or instructed him as his counselor?" the prophet asks (Isa. 40:13–14). Then in the courtroom scene of Isaiah 41 God summons the nations to a world assizes to ascertain whether the nations can determine the future. Their assessment of history rests on only the present and the past, but God controls the future as well, for only he is "the first" and "the last" (Isa. 41:4b). No one can accurately predict what God will do (Isa. 41:26–28)! Isaiah prayed candidly, "Truly you are a God who hides himself" (Isa. 45:15).

Of course, someone might respond that blindness may very well characterize the pagan nations, but surely God's people are in a more privileged position. Be that as it may, the prophet still points out that Israel was blind too. "Who is blind but my servant?" the Lord asks (Isa. 42:19). To the exiles who were waiting for repatriation, God explained, "For my thoughts are not your thoughts, neither are your ways my ways. . . . As the heavens are higher than the earth, so are my ways higher than your ways and my thoughts than your thoughts" (Isa. 55:8–9). If it is suggested that ancient Israel was blind, but the eyesight of modern Christians is better, it must still be pointed out that the New Testament admits a considerable ambiguity about the future. Paul says we know God's final purposes only "in part." At the present we "see but a poor reflection"; only after being clothed with the perfect state shall we "know fully" (1 Cor. 13:9–12). John in a similar vein says, "What we will be has not yet been made known" (1 John 3:2). Christians should take seriously the Olivet Discourse's cautions against speculation. In the end, while Christians have clear advantages over the ancient people of faith because of progressive revelation in the New Testament, they must still be aware of their significant limitations.

Much has been made of biblical statements like Daniel's "None of the wicked will understand, but those who are wise will understand" (Dan. 12:10b), and Amos's "Surely the Sovereign LORD does nothing without revealing his plan to his servants the prophets" (Amos 3:7). However, even here there is need for caution. Daniel's statement follows hard on his being instructed to inquire no further, for full meaning is "closed up and sealed until the time of the end" (Dan. 12:9). Joyce Baldwin is probably correct that the juxtaposition of these two statements indicates that "only after the event can a prophetic word be seen to have been fulfilled."[25] At least there is cause to be wary of the interpretation that prior to the fulfilment of a prediction there will be special exegetical light to which earlier generations were not privy. Amos, on the other hand, does seem to indicate that God's general pattern is to unveil the future through the oracles of the prophets, to which must surely be added the revelations given to Paul and John in the New Testament, not to mention Jesus himself. Still, to recognize that God reveals his future purposes and acts through his prophets is not to say that humans, even the most astute among God's people, have full understanding without ambiguity.

Many elements in biblical prophecy, both Old and New Testament, are ambiguous; it may well be that such ambiguity is intentional, not incidental. That prophetic ambiguity is intentional might be the point of the cryptic passage in the Book of Revelation where John was about to record the utterances of the seven thunders, but was forbidden to do so (Rev. 10:3–4). What is the point in having seven thunders speak but not revealing what they say? This scene suggests that the meaning of the future is still hidden. The counsel of God is always a mystery to some degree, even when it is in the process of being revealed!

Consequently, though interpreters, scholars, and theologians are obliged to study deeply into the themes of eschatology, they cannot by Western rationalism remove the ambiguities that God has allowed. If ambiguity is to any degree intentional in the eschatological passages, then whatever systems are developed and whatever interpretations are advanced must be held loosely and with theological modesty. It may well be that the purpose of biblical prophecy is not to detail the calendar in advance, but to assure God's people that Christ is the sovereign Lord of history. Some details are clear, of course. Jesus is coming! His return will be at an unexpected time! Most other details are less clear.

So does it really matter what views one holds concerning the great tribulation and the millennium? It is probably less important than many Christians think. Let us suppose that the dispensational interpretation is correct, that the church of Jesus Christ will be caught up to heaven, that afterwards there will be a great tribulation for seven years, and at the end there will be a thousand years of peace on earth with the Jews occupying their ancestral lands in Palestine. If that happens, who could possibly argue with God that it should have been some other way? Or suppose the amillennialist is correct. Suppose there is no Jewish millennium. Will some dispensationalist dare to rise up and reprimand God because the land promises were not fulfilled in earthly Palestine to the natural Jew, but in the "better country" to those who have become the children of Abraham by faith and who have received an inheritance in heaven that can never perish, spoil, or fade? Suppose posttribulationism is right, and the church must once again face the onslaught of persecution and martyrdom as did the early church. Could anyone accuse God of reneging on his promises? Are not the power and grace of God that sustained the early church sufficient to do so again? Or suppose all of the eschatological systems are found to be wanting. Is it not possible that God could fulfil some of his predictions in ways that humans have not yet conceived? I suspect that when everything has come to an end, and when every knee bows before Jesus Christ to proclaim him as Lord to the glory of the Father, none of us will be looking around to see if our neighbors are wearing the wrong eschatological hats.

Epilogue

Living in Light of the Lord's Return

If impeccable eschatology is neither mandatory nor possible, what attitudes should Christians cultivate regarding the end? Foremost, they should exhibit a lively expectation of Christ's return. The second coming of Jesus is the blessed hope of the church (Col. 1:27; 1 Tim. 1:1; Titus 1:2; 2:13; 3:7). Even more, the second coming of Jesus is the hope of all creation, which now groans in its present state of decay as it awaits the ultimate freedom God has promised (Rom. 8:18–25). Christians are to eagerly await the coming of God's Son from heaven (1 Thess. 1:10), when they shall be rewarded for their service to the Lord (1 Thess. 2:19–20). And because of this hope believers are to encourage each other, even in the midst of death (1 Thess. 4:18; 5:11).

It is generally true that a lively expectation of Christ's return burns brightest during difficult times. When Christians are comfortable, they are not so apt to think about what is to come, since what they already have seems satisfactory. However, in times of great distress, persecution, and injustice, Christians have always found great solace in the blessed hope of Christ's return. Not surprisingly, then, as the fortunes of God's people increase or decline, the theme of Christ's return ebbs and flows in Christian hymnody and songs.

Second, Christians ought to actively embrace the ethical motivation of the blessed hope. Living a holy life in light of the Lord's return is far more important than any speculation regarding the surrounding events. The ethical motivation was the primary concern in ancient times as well. Daniel concluded his work by saying that in light of God's future "many will be purified, made spotless and refined" (Dan. 12:10a). For all the Hebrew prophets ethical motivation was paramount. Though Jeremiah's call was to announce the uprooting and tearing down of his own nation, his message of doom was not irrevocable. If a prophetic oracle of destruction had been proclaimed, and the nation under judgment repented, the predicted disaster could be averted (Jer. 18:5–10). God's willingness to spare Nineveh is a bright example (Jon. 3:4, 10).

Ethical motivation also accompanies the New Testament's predictions about the second coming of Christ. John wrote, "Everyone who has this hope in him purifies himself, just as he is pure" (1 John 3:3). The hope of Christ's return inspires endurance (1 Thess. 1:3) and urges God's people toward blamelessness (1 Thess. 3:13). In Jesus' parable of the householder on a journey, the servants' uncertainty as to the time of the master's return was a powerful ethical motivation to be busy "each with his assigned task" and to "watch" (Mark 13:32–37). The Greek verb *grēgoreō* ("to watch, be alert") may well carry the force of the Hebrew verb *šāmar* ("to watch, to observe"), which also bears the nuance of taking care of responsibilities. Jesus said, "It will be good for that servant whose master finds him doing so when he returns" (Matt. 24:46). In the same vein, Peter urges his readers to "prepare your minds for action; be self-controlled; set your hope fully on the grace to be given you when Jesus Christ is revealed" (1 Peter 1:13). The question is well put, "What kind of people ought you to be? You ought to live holy and godly lives as you look forward to the day of God" (2 Peter 3:11b–12a).

Finally, the wise Christian should be cautious about speculation. With the change in millennia, speculation is rife. Some point toward "fulfilled signs" that they think mark the time of the church's rapture, others urge the faithful to stock up their underground shelters to wait out the great tribulation, and still others exhibit various stages of panic over everything from microchips to the United Nations. When similarly inadequate responses plagued the Thessalonians, Paul wrote to them that they should not "become easily unsettled or alarmed" (2 Thess. 2:1–2a). After discussing with them some of the traumatic events belonging to the future, Paul reminded them of the Lord's faithfulness and protection against evil, and concluded with the prayer, "Now may the Lord of peace himself give you peace at all times and in every way" (2 Thess. 3:16)!

There is a simplicity of confidence and faith that lies on the other side of complexity. This simplicity is not naivete. It is not the simplicity of the simpleminded, who ask no questions and think no thoughts. Rather, it is the simplicity that, after having looked squarely at the issues and eschatological systems and prognostications, finds peace and stability in the simple assurance that God will keep those whom he calls. It is a simplicity that refuses to substitute secondary things for primary ones. It does not flinch at unanswered questions, and it feels no need to protect a theological ego by becoming the be-all and end-all of eschatological thought. It rests in the ancient confidence of the Hebrew poet, who said, "Therefore we will not fear, though the earth give way and the mountains fall into the heart of the sea" (Ps. 46:2). Babylon may rise and fall, but the city of God, which is "the mother of us all" (Gal. 4:26 KJV), stands secure. "God is within her, she will not fall!" (Ps. 46:5). In this world we "do not have an enduring city, but we are looking for the city that is to come" (Heb. 13:14). And therefore "to him who is able to keep you from falling and to present you before his glorious presence without fault and with great joy—to the only God our Savior be glory, majesty, power and authority, through Jesus Christ our Lord, before all ages, now and forevermore! Amen" (Jude 24–25).

Notes

Introduction

1. There is, of course, the technical question as to whether the new millennium really begins on January 1, 2000, or January 1, 2001 (since there was no year zero), but for our purposes this issue is beside the point. Furthermore, if one is counting from the birth of Jesus and accepts the scholarly conclusion that he was born in about 4 b.c., then the new millennium has begun already. Still, January 1, 2000, has captured the popular imagination, and that is not likely to change.

2. For a more detailed treatment of end-time predictions from ancient times to modern, see Russell Chandler, *Doomsday: The End of the World—A View through Time* (Ann Arbor: Servant, 1993).

3. For assistance in avoiding artificial interpretation see the discussion of literary context in Grant Osborne, *3 Crucial Questions about the Bible* (Grand Rapids: Baker, 1995), 92–95.

Chapter 1: *Are We Living in the Last Days?*

1. Derivatives of six Hebrew words that express the remnant idea are employed over 540 times in the Old Testament. These six words are šā'ar ("to remain, to be left over"), pālaṭ ("to escape, to get away"), mālaṭ ("to escape, to get to safety"), yātar ("to be left over"), śārîd ("survivor"), and 'aḥărît ("remnant"). See Gerhard F. Hasel, "Remnant," in *Interpreter's Dictionary of the Bible,* supplementary volume, ed. Keith Crim (Nashville: Abingdon, 1976), 735.

2. Brevard S. Childs, *Introduction to the Old Testament as Scripture* (Philadelphia: Fortress, 1979), 471, makes the intriguing observation that if the prophecy was conditional, then the prophetic word became the criterion by which to judge history rather than the other way around.

3. Some prophecies seem to have a single fulfilment (e.g., 2 Sam. 12:14b), while others seem to have a near fulfilment as well as a distant fulfilment (e.g., 2 Sam. 7:12–13; 1 Kings 5:5; Luke 1:32–33). Another kind of fulfilment is typological, where one event prefigures a later event (e.g., Exod. 4:22–23; Hos. 11:1; Matt. 2:14–15). While a full discussion of interpretation principles is beyond the scope of this book, one basic principle

is to acknowledge double fulfilments only when there is a direct biblical explanation.

4. The singling out of the four Songs of the Servant is a product of nineteenth-century scholarship. They are oracles which depict the mission of the 'Ebed-Yahweh (Isa. 42:1–4), his call (Isa. 49:1–6), his submission to the divine purpose (Isa. 50:4–9), and his humiliation and ultimate exaltation (Isa. 52:13–53:12). See C. R. North, "The Servant of the Lord," in *Interpreter's Dictionary of the Bible,* ed. George A. Buttrick, 4 vols. (Nashville: Abingdon, 1962), 4:292–94.

5. Most commentators apply Isa. 49:7 to the collective servant, but particularly in light of the fourth Servant Song (Isa. 52:13–53:12), the passage probably refers to the individual servant. Jesus was, of course, despised and abhorred, and under Pilate, Herod, and Caesar lived as a servant of rulers. See G. W. Grogan, "Isaiah," in *Expositor's Bible Commentary,* ed. Frank E. Gaebelein, 12 vols. (Grand Rapids: Zondervan, 1986), 6:285.

6. The term "Sinim" (v. 12) is unclear. It might refer to Aswan, Egypt. Some Hebrew scholars identify it with the Chinese. In either case, the point is to refer to people from the far-off lands of the world.

7. The Septuagint follows a lesser meaning of *nāzāh* ("to amaze or startle") instead of the more usual meaning ("to sprinkle"). This lesser meaning is followed by several English versions as well (RSV, NEB, NAB, ASVmg, NKJVmg, NIVmg), though not all (NIV, ASV, KJV, NKJV). The translators who make this choice deem that it fits the context better than does a priestly image. However, the priestly nuance seems to be equally appropriate in light of the vicarious suffering and intercession described later (Isa. 53:10, 12b).

8. F. F. Bruce, *The Epistle to the Hebrews,* New International Commentary on the New Testament (Grand Rapids: Eerdmans, 1964), 3.

9. Joachim Jeremias, *New Testament Theology* (New York: Scribner, 1971), 80–82.

10. For a sustained defense of this interpretation, see David P. Moessner, *Lord of the Banquet: The Literary and Theological Significance of the Lukan Travel Narrative* (Minneapolis: Fortress, 1989), 264–77.

11. It is now widely accepted that the phrases "kingdom of heaven" (in Matthew's Gospel) and "kingdom of God" (in the other Gospels) refer to the same thing, Matthew preferring to use a more Jewish-sensitive term given the rabbinical reluctance to refer to God directly. In Jewish rabbinic literature the common phrase is "the kingdom of the heavens."

12. The translation of this passage can be either "within you" or "among you," but in either case it directly suggests the presence of the kingdom.

13. For more extensive discussion see George Eldon Ladd, *Crucial Questions about the Kingdom of God* (Grand Rapids: Eerdmans, 1952).

14. Archibald M. Hunter, *The Gospel according to St. Paul* (Philadelphia: Westminster, 1966), 14–57.

Chapter 2: *Should Christians Try to Predict Christ's Return?*

1. For a full treatment of Jewish apocalyptic thought and interpretation, see D. S. Russell, *The Method and Message of Jewish Apocalyptic* (Philadelphia: Westminster, 1964). For a complete edition of apocalyptic works, see James H. Charlesworth, ed., *The Old Testament Pseudepigrapha,* 2 vols. (Garden City, N.Y.: Doubleday, 1983, 1985).

2. Lactantius *Divine Institutes* 7.25.

3. Irenaeus *Against Heresies* 5.23.2; Lactantius *Divine Institutes* 7.14; Methodius, "Extracts from the Work 'On Things Created,'" *Fragments,* ix.

4. Clarence Larkin, *Dispensational Truth,* 3d ed. (Philadelphia: Clarence Larkin, 1920), 16–17.

5. Derek Kidner, *Psalms 73–150* (Downers Grove, Ill.: InterVarsity, 1975), 329.

6. For a full exploration of the local contexts of these congregations in the ancient world, see the classic study by William M. Ramsay, *The Letters to the Seven Churches* (Grand Rapids: Baker, 1979 reprint), or, more recently, Colin J. Hemer, *Letters to the Seven Churches of Asia in Their Local Setting* (Sheffield: JSOT, 1986).

7. R. T. France, *Matthew,* Tyndale New Testament Commentaries (Grand Rapids: Eerdmans, 1985), 339.

8. Loraine Boettner, *The Millennium* (Philadelphia: Presbyterian and Reformed, 1957), 22, 29.

9. Ernest R. Sandeen, *The Roots of Fundamentalism: British and American Millenarianism, 1800–1930* (Grand Rapids: Baker, 1978 reprint), 5–7.

10. The entire story of Darby's influence can be found in Clarence B. Bass, *Backgrounds to Dispensationalism: Its Historical Genesis and Ecclesiastical Implications* (Grand Rapids: Eerdmans, 1960).

11. Hal Lindsey with C. C. Carlson, *The Late Great Planet Earth* (Grand Rapids: Zondervan, 1970), 53–54.

12. George Eldon Ladd, *The Last Things* (Grand Rapids: Eerdmans, 1978), 28.

13. Grant R. Osborne, *The Hermeneutical Spiral* (Downers Grove, Ill.: InterVarsity, 1991), 227.

Chapter 3: *What Must Christians Believe about the Last Days?*

1. What is described here is the well-known version of dispensationalism popular among laypersons and generally defined by the Scofield Reference Bible. To color all dispensationalists with the same brush, however, is unfair. Among dispensational scholars there has been considerable development in eschatological thought, much of it away from the popular dispensational tenets. See the two-part article by Craig A. Blaising, "Doctrinal Development in Orthodoxy," *Bibliotheca Sacra* 145, no. 578 (1988): 133–40, and "Development of Dispensationalism by Contemporary Dispensationalists," *Bibliotheca Sacra* 145, no. 579 (1988): 254–80; and Craig A. Blaising and Darrell L. Bock, *Progressive Dispensationalism* (Wheaton, Ill.: Victor, 1993). This development has not as yet made a significant impact on the large mass of popular dispensationalists who still articulate their theology in the old way. For an insightful dialogue between dispensationalists and nondispensationalists, see Vern S. Poythress, *Understanding Dispensationalism,* 2d ed. (Phillipsburg, N.J.: Presbyterian and Reformed, 1994).

2. See the note to the heading at Gen. 1:28, *New Scofield Reference Bible* (Oxford: Oxford University Press, 1967), 3.

3. C. I. Scofield, *Rightly Dividing the Word of Truth* (New York: Revell, 1907).

4. In fact, the term *Heilsgeschichte* includes nonevangelical scholars, such as Oscar Cullmann and Joachim Jeremias, as well as evangelical scholars, although our treatment will be confined to the evangelical concept of salvation-history. Evangelicals who generally seem to fall into the salvation-history school include George Eldon Ladd, I. Howard Marshall, Herman Ridderbos, Leonhard Goppelt, Robert Mounce, Geerhardus Vos, F. F. Bruce, and R. K. Harrison.

5. To be sure, progressive dispensationalists have been won over to the position of inaugurated eschatology, but it remains to be seen if they will significantly impact their dispensational peers; see Blaising and Bock, *Progressive Dispensationalism,* 162, 209, 248–62.

6. John F. Walvoord, *Daniel: The Key to Prophetic Revelation* (Chicago: Moody, 1971).

7. Dispensationalists are careful to use the third decree as their starting point in

order to make their calculations work. (There were two earlier decrees permitting the restoration of Jerusalem, one by Cyrus in 538 B.C. [Ezra 1:2–4] and one by Artaxerxes in 458 B.C. [Ezra 7:11–26].) A critical consideration in the dispensationalist calculations is the biblical use of lunar years rather than our present solar years.

8. William Hendriksen, *Mark* (Grand Rapids: Baker, 1975), 526–28; D. A. Carson, "Matthew," in *Expositor's Bible Commentary,* ed. Frank E. Gaebelein, 12 vols. (Grand Rapids: Zondervan, 1984), 8:491–95; R. T. France, *Matthew,* Tyndale New Testament Commentaries (Grand Rapids: Eerdmans, 1985), 333–36.

9. George Eldon Ladd, *A Theology of the New Testament* (Grand Rapids: Eerdmans, 1974), 196–99.

10. Robert H. Gundry, *The Church and the Tribulation* (Grand Rapids: Zondervan, 1973), 76, 83, 91; Ladd, *Theology,* 197–98.

11. A prime example of this failure is John F. Walvoord, *The Rapture Question* (Findlay, Ohio: Dunham, 1957), 56–60, 192.

12. E. Peterson, "ἀπάντησις [apantēsis]," in *Theological Dictionary of the New Testament,* ed. G. Kittel and G. Friedrich, trans. Geoffrey W. Bromiley, 10 vols. (Grand Rapids: Eerdmans, 1964–76), 1:380–81; W. Mundle, "καταντάω [katantaō]," in *New International Dictionary of New Testament Theology,* ed. Colin Brown, 4 vols. (Grand Rapids: Zondervan, 1975–86), 1:325.

13. George Eldon Ladd, *The Blessed Hope* (Grand Rapids: Eerdmans, 1956), 19–31.

14. For two evangelical idealist interpretations of Revelation see William Milligan, *The Book of Revelation,* Expositor's Bible (London: Hodder and Stoughton, 1909); and, more recently, Michael Wilcock, *I Saw Heaven Opened: The Message of Revelation* (Downers Grove, Ill.: InterVarsity, 1975).

15. Examples of the historicist view may be seen in Matthew Henry, *Matthew Henry's Commentary on the Whole Bible,* 6 vols. (Old Tappan, N.J.: Revell, n.d.); and Adam Clarke, *Clarke's Commentary,* 6 vols. (Nashville: Abingdon, n.d.). Though not a commentary on the Book of Revelation, the popular *Fox's Book of Martyrs,* ed. W. B. Forbush (Grand Rapids: Zondervan, 1978 reprint), is a favorite source for historicist interpretation, as is Alexander Hislop, *The Two Babylons,* 2d ed. (Neptune, N.J.: Loizeaux, 1959).

16. A very readable example of preterist interpretation is William Barclay, *The Revelation of John,* 2 vols. (Philadelphia: Westminster, 1976).

17. A representative dispensational interpretation of the Book of Revelation is John F. Walvoord, *The Revelation of Jesus Christ* (Chicago: Moody, 1966).

18. For a historic premillennial commentary see George Eldon Ladd, *A Commentary on the Revelation of John* (Grand Rapids: Eerdmans, 1972).

19. Irenaeus *Against Heresies* 5.30.3 (Irenaeus's works date from the last quarter of the second century).

20. David F. Wright, "What the First Christians Believed," in *Eerdmans' Handbook to the History of Christianity,* ed. Tim Dowley (Grand Rapids: Eerdmans, 1977), 113.

21. Ibid., 115.

22. Justo L. Gonzales, *A History of Christian Thought,* 3 vols. (Nashville: Abingdon, 1970), 1:102.

23. Justin Martyr *Dialogue with Trypho* 80.

24. Adam Clarke, *Clarke's Commentary,* 6 vols. (New York: Abingdon, n.d.), 6:965.

25. Joyce Baldwin, *Daniel: An Introduction and Commentary* (Downers Grove, Ill.: InterVarsity, 1978), 208.

Glossary

The study of prophecy has received a tremendous amount of attention, especially in the past century and a half, which in turn has produced a rather large amount of jargon. It is almost impossible to talk about this subject without using at least some of this jargon. One of the stated goals of the 3 Crucial Questions series is to avoid such special language and technical terms, but in this case a brief glossary is advisable.

Abomination of desolation. A phrase used by Daniel (9:27; 11:31; 12:11) to denote the defilement of the temple and later referred to by Christ (Matt. 24:15; Mark 13:14).

Allegory. A figurative expression in which seemingly obvious elements are symbols of something deeper.

Amillennialism. The view that there will be no future utopian age of one thousand years within history. The present kingdom of God will be immediately superseded by the eternal state without an intervening age.

Apocalyptic. A body of intertestamental Jewish writings (later followed by similar Christian writings) which describe the end of the age in cataclysmic, highly symbolic terms.

Dispensationalism. A conservative theology which stresses the difference between two peoples of God, Israel and the Christian church. Pretribulational and premillennial, it traditionally divides human history into seven distinct eras, though modern dispensationalists sometimes opt for three distinct eras.

Epiphany. In eschatological contexts, the manifestation of Christ at his second advent.

Eschatology. Literally "discourse about the last things," that part of Christian teaching concerned with the end of human history. Traditionally, it has encompassed such matters as the second coming of Christ, the resurrection of the dead, the immortality of the soul, the final judgment, and the future states of heaven and hell.

Eschatology, Inaugurated. The view that with the first advent of Christ the kingdom of God broke into the world, though in a partial and hidden way; the consummation of the kingdom of God will be at the second advent.

Historicism. Interpretation of the Book of Revelation as a symbolic representation of church history, particularly the struggles between the Roman and Protestant churches in the Reformation. Historicism as described here should not be confused with the conclusions of Ernst Troeltsch (1865–1923), who grappled with problems raised by the scientific historical method.

Idealism. Nonliteral, spiritual interpretation of the Book of Revelation as an allegory of the struggle between good and evil, God's people against the powers of Satan.

Imminence. With reference to the events of the end times, the possibility of occurrence at any moment. For dispensationalists the word refers specifically to the rapture; for nondispensationalists it refers to the complex of events surrounding the second advent (nondispensationalists also speak of these events as "impending").

Midtribulationism. The belief in the futurity of the seventieth week of Daniel with the rapture of the church occurring after the first three-and-a-half years (a view defended especially by the late J. Oliver Buswell of Wheaton College).

Millenarianism (also **Millennialism**). The belief that there will be a future utopian age, usually thought of as a thousand years in length.

Noneschatological interpretation. The view that the Bible or parts thereof do not predict the future in general nor end-time events in particular.

Parousia. New Testament Greek word referring to the coming or presence of Christ in his second advent.

Postmillennialism. The belief that the second advent of Christ will occur after worldwide conversion to Christianity and a resultant utopian age (this view is sometimes associated with scientific and cultural advancement).

Posttribulationism. The belief that the rapture of the church will occur after the period of affliction at the end of the present age.

It is sometimes, but not always, associated with the end of the seventieth week of Daniel.

Premillennialism. The belief that the second advent of Christ will result directly in an age of utopia. It looks for the consummation of the kingdom of God to occur within history rather than beyond it.

Premillennialism, Historic. The belief in a future millennium within history as the consummation of the kingdom of God following the second advent of Christ. Posttribulational, this view is deemed "historic" because it reflects the premillennialism of the postapostolic church.

Pretribulationism. The belief that the church will be raptured out of the world prior to the great tribulation, i.e., the seventieth week of Daniel. This view is necessary to preserve the dispensational belief that there are two peoples of God. Before God can deal with his national people, Israel, whom he has temporarily set aside, he must remove from the world his spiritual people, the church.

Rapture. The "catching up" of believers into the air to meet Christ when he returns (the term comes from the Latin Vulgate of 1 Thess. 4:17).

Tribulation. A time of intense affliction in the world as predicted by Christ (Matt. 24:21 and parallels). In dispensationalism it coincides with the seventieth week of Daniel as the climax of the present age.

Typology. The study of persons, things, or events in the Old Testament that prefigure a truth in the New Testament. Some interpreters accept typology only where the New Testament directly confirms it; others engage in typology with or without New Testament confirmation as a way of Christianizing the Old Testament.

Annotated Bibliography

Bass, Clarence B. *Backgrounds to Dispensationalism: Its Historical Genesis and Ecclesiastical Implications.* Grand Rapids: Eerdmans, 1960.

> Any contemporary student of eschatology must address the system of dispensationalism, whether one embraces it or not, since it is the most popular interpretive system among fundamentalists. This work explores dispensationalism's nineteenth-century origin in England, and especially the development of its distinctives under the guidance of its primary founder, John Nelson Darby.

Boyer, Paul. *When Time Shall Be No More.* Cambridge, Mass.: Harvard University Press, 1992.

> This sociological assessment of the impact which prophetic beliefs have had on American culture moves the discussion beyond theological theory to pragmatic effect. The American religious fascination with end-time prophecy has had a much wider influence on contemporary culture than most people realize. Exploring the social implications of this "theology of the people," Boyer documents its impact well.

Bright, John. *The Kingdom of God.* Nashville: Abingdon, 1953.

> This work of biblical theology rather than eschatology includes considerable critical discussion which espouses viewpoints incompatible with conservative evangelical belief in the inerrancy of Scripture. Nevertheless, Bright makes sense of the flow of Old Testament thought and its connection to the New Testament. His work, as well as any other in print, addresses the prophets in the milieu of their own times and prepares the student of the Bible to read the prophetic passages in the way the first readers read them. In this sense it is indispensable.

147

Chandler, Russell. *Doomsday: The End of the World—A View through Time.* Ann Arbor: Servant, 1993.

> "End-time fever" is not a new phenomenon. Through the centuries the faithful have exhibited a fascination with the end of the world and a propensity to speculate about how the end will come. Discussing past individuals, groups, and theories concerned with the end times, this book provides perspective as modern Christians engage in the same sort of speculation.

Clouse, Robert G., ed. *The Meaning of the Millennium: Four Views.* Downers Grove, Ill.: InterVarsity, 1977.

> Each of the four predominant millennial views is discussed by an evangelical proponent. George Eldon Ladd addresses the millennial question from the standpoint of historic premillennialism, as does Herman Hoyt from the dispensational position, Loraine Boettner postmillennialism, and Anthony Hoekema amillennialism. Each interacts with the views of the others in addition to explaining his own position.

Cullmann, Oscar. *Christ and Time.* Translated by Floyd V. Filson. Revised ed. Philadelphia: Westminster, 1964.

> This seminal work explores the New Testament's vocabulary for time, the nuances of which are critical if one is to appreciate the New Testament writers' understanding of the Christ event within the context of human history and in light of the predictions of the Hebrew prophets. Cullmann develops a clear understanding of the overlapping of the ages (i.e., the beginning of the new age before the conclusion of the old age).

Erickson, Millard J. *Contemporary Options in Eschatology.* Grand Rapids: Baker, 1977.

> This work has the merit of treating not only the various millennial views, but also the various tribulational and nonevangelical views of eschatology. Thus the reader surveys not only the pretribulational and posttribulational positions, but also the systems of realized eschatology, existential eschatology, and the theology of hope which arose in the context of the "death of God" movement. Though somewhat dated, it is still quite useful in surveying the major distinctives of the various positions.

Ladd, George Eldon. *The Blessed Hope.* Grand Rapids: Eerdmans, 1956.

> While the position espoused, historic premillennialism, was not new, this work broke new ground in the middle of the twentieth century by departing from the dispensationalism which had become standard among fundamentalists and many evangelicals.

Ladd argues for a premillennial, posttribulational position more in line with the beliefs of the early Fathers of the Christian church.

———. *The Presence of the Future.* Grand Rapids: Eerdmans, 1974.

A seminal work on the nature of the kingdom of God as preached by Jesus in the Gospels, this book explains what is sometimes called inaugurated eschatology, that is, the approach that views the kingdom of God as both present and future. The kingdom was inaugurated by Christ in his earthly ministry, but it will not be consummated until his second coming. Ladd's study not only takes into account the biblical material, but also interacts with Jewish apocalyptic material.

Morris, Leon. *Apocalyptic.* Grand Rapids: Eerdmans, 1972.

Though not as comprehensive as D. S. Russell's *Method and Message of Jewish Apocalyptic,* this short, readable evangelical introduction to apocalyptic literature will assist the nonprofessional in identifying the major characteristics of apocalyptic style.

Sandeen, Ernest R. *The Roots of Fundamentalism: British and American Millenarianism, 1800–1930.* Grand Rapids: Baker, 1978 reprint.

In some ways similar to Bass's *Backgrounds to Dispensationalism,* this book is much broader in its assessment of the development of eschatological views within the nineteenth and twentieth centuries. It is the standard history on the development of modern premillennial thought.

General Index

Abomination of desolation, 110, 111, 143
Abraham, seed of, 58, 85
Abrahamic covenant, 19, 21, 25, 27, 31, 36, 45–46, 58, 80, 95
Adam, 93–94
Age, church: assumption of lengthy, 62, 63; calculating the length of the, 73–78
Ages, theory of church, 74–76
Alexander the Great, 106
Allegorical interpretation: of the seven churches, 75–76; of Revelation, 116–17
Allegory, 143
Already/not yet, 66–67
Ambiguity of New Testament language, 87, 131–32
Amillennialism, 17, 85, 94, 100, 104, 126–27, 143
Amos, 22, 30–31
Anabaptists, 72
Anathoth, field of, 38
Anna, 52
Antichrist, 15, 70, 95, 106, 107, 108, 116, 124
Apantēsis, 114
Apocalyptic: Jewish, 70–71, 116, 117; Christian, 71–73
Apocalyptic literature, 44, 87, 121, 143
Apokalypsis, 66, 91–92, 115
Apostles' Creed, 129
Aristides, 128, 129
Artaxerxes, 107
Augustine, 98

Babylon, 49, 106
Baldwin, Joyce, 132

Beast of Revelation, 117, 124
Bengel, J. A., 98
Biblical theology, 17–18, 98
Birth narratives, 50–52
Blessed hope, ethical motivation of the, 135–36
Blessings and cursings, 20, 21–22, 38. *See also* Deuteronomic code
Branch, 36–37, 39, 43
British millenarianism, 79
Bruce, F. F., 50
Bullinger, Heinrich, 93
Buswell, J. Oliver, 144

Calvin, John, 93
Calvinism, five points of, 94
Camping, Harold, 16
Canaan, conquest of, 19, 20
Carchemish, 32
Carson, D. A., 110
China, 81–82, 86
Christ event. *See* Jesus event
Christian apocalyptic, 71–73
Christian perspective of Hebrew prophecy, 49–50
Church age: assumption of lengthy, 62, 63; calculating the length of the, 73–78
Church ages, theory of, 74–76
Church and Israel in dispensationalism, dichotomy between, 80, 93, 94, 95, 96–97, 101, 102, 143, 145
Clarke, Adam, 130
Common Market, 15, 82
Communism, 81–82, 86

151

Scripture Index

Daniel J. Lewis is senior pastor of Troy Christian Chapel in Troy, Michigan. A former college professor, he currently serves on the adjunct faculty of William Tyndale College and has authored over forty monographs on biblical themes and numerous articles for scholarly and professional publications.